The Business of Trust

By Ray Filasky

Copyright © 2014 Ray Filasky

All Rights Reserved

Fools think their own way is right, but the wise listen to advice.
(Proverbs 12:15)

The Business of Trust

I suspect few would argue that we live in a society that has lost much of its trust for politicians, law enforcement, clergy, bankers, sales people, and quite frankly business in general. It is difficult to pinpoint when exactly the scales began to tip, but we find ourselves in a time where it is difficult to move forward on most any front as each side is afraid to trust the other's motives and sincerity. Even when both sides can agree on the appropriate course of action neither is willing to allow the other the satisfaction of being right for fear of being positioned as the "loser" in the fight. Politicians are afraid it will give their opponents a leg up in the next election, law enforcement officials refuse to appear weak in a tough environment of crime, clergy actually promote divisiveness as a means to fill their pews rather than those of another denomination, and business people of all types pursue personal and corporate agendas at the expense of what is best for their employees, customers and investors.

Are we afraid of being wrong, or is it just that we are often misguided in our thinking? One of the very first business oriented books I have read is "The Peter Principle" written in 1969 by Dr. Lawrence J. Peter and Raymond Hull. Although I have forgotten many of the details of the book, the key point of the argument was that we all, at some point in our careers, reach our level of incompetence. We may be exceptional at one level in an organization and consequently promoted to a higher level for which we may not be at all suited, thereby delivering lackluster performance but too good to be demoted to our initial position.

Unfortunately, it is rarely ever uncovered because of-times we are being evaluated by someone who has also reached their level of incompetence. Let me postulate, if I may, that or ability to trust reacts much the same way. We all have some baseline level of trust cultivated by our childhood experiences, our education, and our work / life encounters. We will typically trust others to the extent that we have encountered trustworthiness in most people but certainly not more than the level of trustworthiness we find in ourselves. Our inability to trust creates an atmosphere of decreasing expectations regarding our ability to have confidence in the motives of others.

Now, you may ask, why is trust so important in business? Isn't even the foundation for much of Business Law predicated on the concept of "caveat emptor" (let the buyer beware)? Of course being trustworthy is the moral imperative, but we are now talking about "in the trenches" – competitive business activity. Where does trust fall in the pecking order of profits, investor returns, personal enrichment, or business survival. I firmly believe that by creating an atmosphere of trust the business enterprise can bring out the best in its employees and foster a mutually beneficial relationship with all its stakeholders.

The effective manager of today will nurture that level of trust and free up the creative energies of their workforce as employees willingly share their best ideas rather than being more concerned with, watching their back, building their own "personal brand" or looking for the next good job. Other stakeholders such as vendors and service providers will be less likely to build in quite so high a risk premium in their pricing to protect them against the things they are sure you are not disclosing and financial partners will be less suspicious of poor business decisions made only to avoid breaking a lending covenant thereby insuring lower rates or less restrictive covenants in the future.

It is my desire that this book will serve as a primer for new managers in hopes that their career can make a difference in the lives of all those they supervise, influence or encounter. Additionally, the concepts put forth are intended to be a "gut check" for the experienced manager challenging them to re-evaluate their motivation and approach to the workplace. In either case, managers that can rebuild the atmosphere of mutual trust between business, employees, and stakeholders will not only deliver sustainable profits, but will build lasting value as businesses become more aware of the real threat to their success – stifling the entrepreneurial spirit of their employees.

Table of Contents

Introduction 10
Why is management so important? 14
    Evaluate current circumstances: 15
    Anticipate changing market forces: 19
    Craft a strategic course of action: 22
    Provide for its implementation: 24
    Champion the effort: 28
    Recognize the contribution of others: 30
Pollyanna Doesn't Live Here Anymore 33
    Why is it important to trust others? 34
    Why is it important that others trust you? 37
    Help others look good until they get good: 39
    Take a good look in the mirror: 41
Demonstrating Trust in People 44
    Clearing away the obstacles: 45
    Confide in your employees – share the data: 48
    Creating the right expectations: 50
    Measuring performance appropriately: 55
    Give credit where credit is due: 61
    Address weaknesses compassionately: 64
    Strongly support continuous learning: 71
    Challenge growth and adapting to change: 74
    Make the tough call when all else fails: 78

Cultivating Trust in Management Decisions 87
    Senior managers must have the trust of the people: 88
    Process improvement must involve those who are actually doing it: 91
    Stay abreast of changing industry dynamics: 95
    Live up to your commitments: 103
    Management Perks: 108
    Don't assume everyone knows: 110
    Don't assume you know it all: 112
Create an Organization That Can Be Trusted 117
    Be caring and consistent with employees: 118
    Be responsive to the community: 121
    Be careful with "spin": 124
    Build mutual respect with vendors: 126
    Communicate effectively: 131
Too Much Management 137
    Creating urgency without frustration: 143
    Choose your battles: 147
    Not everything can be done at the same time: 150
Hiring the Right People is Essential 155
    First Impressions Can Mislead You: 156
    Institutional Knowledge Matters: 158
    Adaptability is a Must: 162
    What Message Have you Sent? 165
There is No Free Lunch 169
    There will be push-back: 170

Think before you hit send: 177
Swallow your pride: 179
Getting even is a luxury you can't afford: 184
Do the right things for the right reasons: 188
Conclusion 200
About the Author: 207

Introduction

The business curriculum at most schools today seems focused on training the next Fortune 500 C.E.O. yet the vast majority of students will go on to be front-line or mid-level managers. It is like structuring the game plan for a Pop-Warner football team around one designed for the NFL. The number of individuals that will actually make it that far is incalculably small; most will enjoy the game at the little league level, some will continue on through high school and an ever-shrinking number will play in college but no further. (In a recent article for USA Today, Gary Mihoces indicated that there are 3.5 million youngsters playing youth football, 1.3 million playing in High School another 100,000 at the College level, but a mere 2,000 at the professional level.) Just as the astute coach will enable those youngsters to enjoy the game at whatever level they will be playing, it would make sense for educators to assist business students in their ability to be good front-line managers first and give them a sense of why that is so important.

I ask you to think for a moment about what factors most contribute to the contentment of an employee; what makes them reasonably happy or gives them a sense of fulfillment on the job? First there are what 20th century philosopher and business professor Frederick Herzberg referred to as hygienic factors, those things such as wages and benefits that were not so much motivators as they are necessary benefits to attract and retain the required level of expertise for a particular job. These areas of compensation are essentially table stakes if an employer wishes to maintain certain skill sets in-house. Beyond that, however, there are various other aspects of the job that engage, enrich or motivate an individual and, conversely, discourage or disillusion team members when they are lacking. It is my contention that the most influential of these is one's immediate supervisor.

Regardless of the qualities of any particular entity, there are those within it that conduct themselves in ways that are almost contradictory to the overall personality of the organization. When this happens to be in a supervisory position, it can be extremely detrimental to the individuals within that department or business unit as well as the entire organization. Those Individuals who are at odds with this type of manager will find themselves frustrated and unappreciated as previously successful and rewarded methods are criticized. This is typically because the supervisor in question is either new to the organization or at least new to this particular unit and lacks the first-hand knowledge of the inner workings of the department or the underlying skills necessary to get the job done. This feeling of exasperation seems to fester within the unit, affecting the most productive and experienced employees the most. Left unaddressed, this atmosphere leads to staff members leaving the company for different jobs, taking early retirement or at the very least hurting productivity.

On the company level, this situation can cause irreparable harm before it is even detected. By the time senior managers recognize the friction the company may have already lost or alienated some very talented individuals, after all the most talented are less apt to tolerate such treatment and find it easiest to obtain another position. Ironically, the defections can happen so slowly they almost fly under the radar, masked by other business developments resulting in more extensive damage to the team morale as they are exposed for longer periods of time to the friction. Even when the situation is eventually fixed (and they do get fixed), team members are much more skeptical and less trusting of subsequent managers thereby making future transitions slower and unnecessarily difficult.

Besides the actual cost in human talent and productivity, there is the hidden and less quantifiable expense of lost initiative. A friend of mine once said in frustration: "If we have so many people focusing solely on where we have been, who the heck is watching where we are going?" When we create an atmosphere that lacks trust, employees lose the confidence to innovate – to be creative. Leaders will never get more than they expected from staff members who are dependent on the next punch list for direction. Only when employees are given the freedom to think for themselves, the latitude to learn from an occasional mistake and to implement workable solutions will they develop the skills necessary think on their feet. It is that drive to be innovative, the passion for one's job that is foundational for great organizations.

It is for these reasons that this book is written, that it might influence even the smallest number of current and future managers. A single manager, even at an entry level, may supervise a few hundred people during the course of their career and, as a result, have the opportunity to enrich their lives with a feeling of self-worth and contribution. All of us like to make a difference and will give our utmost to do so. The very best companies have discovered the value of engaged, passionate and innovative employees whose personal success is in concert with the aspirations of the organization.

Why is management so important?

Most of us, at some point in our careers, have experienced or witnessed errors in judgment on the part of managers at various levels (Maybe I'm being slightly diplomatic). These have been demoralizing encounters, resulting from inexperience or possibly just plain arrogance and entitlement on the part of a misguided supervisor. Whether this happens at the senior management level, mid-level or the front line supervisor we can find evidence of the disastrous effect it has on financial performance and company morale. We rely on our leaders to evaluate current circumstances, anticipate changing market forces, craft a strategic course of action, provide for its implementation, champion the effort, and recognize those that are making positive contributions toward the attainment of these goals. The challenge, of course, is that all these must take place in concert and that rarely do we find leadership that well-coordinated. The reality is that most of us are stronger at some things than we are at others, but all good managers understand that just because they are weak at something does not mean that it is unnecessary. The best leaders find ways to accomplish those things that are important and staff to their weaknesses. They find ways to employ individuals who fill the gaps, so to speak, in their strengths thereby insuring that critical areas of performance are not ignored and cultivating an element of trust among all concerned. Let's take a look at some of those leadership expectations.

Evaluate current circumstances:

One would assume it elementary that a clear understanding of the existing organizational culture, its strengths, and its weaknesses is necessary if a plan is to be formulated for any future endeavor, not to mention a clear understanding of external influences as well. All too frequently, however, we find managers who are so focused on their own personal vision they ignore the existing platform from which they must launch any initiative. Leaders who "believe in their own hype" frequently fail to engage those actually doing the job, the very people with the first-hand knowledge of what it takes to get the job done; opting instead to believe that they know best. Let me be clear, there are times when a new direction must be taken and change is rarely ever easy or wholeheartedly embraced, but if we can't communicate the merits of these changes successfully to the very people who have to get the work done then how on earth will we ever translate the changes into a better relationship with our customers and stakeholders?

A corporate Vice President I worked for some years back made a statement that I have always found helpful when attempting to put in perspective the importance of involving the right people in the plan. "We must find a way to get from here to there and take both our customers and our employees with us." There are times when change is critical to the survival of a business or instances when it is just a natural progression of the current offering, but even if the plan is to be something entirely different in ten years, creating a solid foundation for that change is imperative. Wells Fargo no longer handles business via stagecoach and pony express, but they do handle express banking electronically; IBM no longer produces typewriters, but they do process information; the movie industry no longer has to get you to leave your home and drive to a theater, but they still sell their movies - they just stream them into your homes or mobile device on demand. Change is inevitable and can only happen when people work together in an atmosphere of trust and respect bringing it to fruition.

    A clear understanding of the current organizational dynamics, key revenue contributors, and where important institutional knowledge resides will enable senior managers to involve the right people, embrace realistic expectations, and better plan sequential steps toward the ultimate goal. It is often said that people do not like change. I am not sure that change in and of itself is the demon, but rather frustration and marginalization. Effective leaders build trust with employees by understanding their contribution, respecting their particular skill set regardless of societal valuation, and seeking input. Most employees truly want to do a good job and attempt to do so within the parameters of the information they have been given. They resent insignificance and rebel against that which seems counterproductive, at times exhibiting a misguided work ethic as they strive very hard at what they firmly believe to be the correct course of action even if it is at odds with a well thought out strategic plan.

An old business school quote rings very true; "People tend to support only that which they help to create." When managers take the time to thoroughly understand the strengths and weaknesses of their team, they are better able to formulate successful plans. Just as any good coach adapts his or her game plan to the various strengths of their players, or a symphony director positons their musicians to enhance the performance, a manager needs to develop plans that best uses the talents within their group. At times it means acquiring additional skills that are not currently present or possibly discovering untapped talents within one's own unit. The key point is that a plan needs a reasonable chance of success or else it is just foolhardy. To embark on some grandiose project without first assessing the existing talent pool is not just a prescription for failure but also has a demoralizing and detrimental effect on the staff. Getting to know team members and their obvious (and not so obvious) capabilities will not only result in clearer insight with regards to the scope of any potential project, but it will also begin to develop a more cohesive team as they feel engaged and appreciated.

This goes for relevant stakeholders also; such as investors, lenders or vendors who value well thought out company direction and continuity of effort. Poorly communicated and executed initiatives result in performance hiccups that have a way of sending the wrong message to other entities that play a significant role in the success of the organization. By way of example, let me relate an illustration I witnessed first-hand. I was the operations manager for a business unit that consistently delivered good profitability and return on capital. During a time of financial stress for the parent company, an unsolicited offer to buy this segment of the business was presented. Of course, during times of hardship, the quick fix of a cash infusion looks very attractive and we accepted a Letter of Intent and moved into the due diligence phase. The process was moving along at a rapid pace as facilities were inspected and financials validated. It was apparent to those of us most closely involved that the purchaser had undervalued our business unit and was attempting to obtain it well under market value, a fact that seemed to be off the radar screen of the parent company in their zeal to complete the deal. To everyone's surprise, however, the private equity fund being used by the purchaser recognized that this deal required a greater investment than they will typically approve for a single acquisition and backed out causing the purchaser to seek another equity partner. This hesitation on their part resulted in the parent company being convinced by their consultants in the meantime that too much EBITA would go away with the sale of that unit and the deal was canceled. Although this was a blessing for our company and all of us involved, it was an example of how misinformation to key stakeholders can result in problems.

Likewise, the opinion any of these stakeholders have of your organization may weigh heavily during times of financials uncertainty or industry upheaval. It is the confidence they have in your company that will convince them to stay with you even during a tough stretch. There can be times when capital availability is tight and a firm must rely more heavily on the payment terms of its suppliers or the willingness of lenders to maintain the existing lines of credit. Having a thorough understanding of the status of these relationships is necessary if one is to construct any major plan of action, not to mention the expertise some of these stakeholders may bring to the table free of charge because they feel your company's success is mutually beneficial.

Anticipate changing market forces:

For the most part managers are put in place because they have demonstrated superior understanding of their business and the ability to get things done. Unfortunately, the very things that were necessary and contributed to their promotion may well change before their first performance appraisal. Far too many managers ascribe to the statement (excuse the liberties taken with the title to Robert Fulghum's book) "All I Really Need to Know I learned in Business School" or at least in my first managerial assignment. Certainly experience is invaluable and should be weighted heavily in any decision process, but just as the opportunities and obstacles are continuously changing so are the tools to deal with them. It becomes imperative that managers look objectively at the changing landscape and recognize their own blind-spots. Life-long learning is not just a buzzword for continuing education; it is an imperative for anyone who wishes to remain relevant and to bring positive contribution to the workplace. As in all generations past, the trendsetters of today will always be at risk of being the dinosaurs of tomorrow.

Please understand that market forces are not confined only to one's particular industry (although that is extremely important and I will discuss in a moment) but refers to all manner of social, cultural, environmental, and technological changes.

Sociologists point out that we have generational groupings that have certain tendencies making them different than those before or after them. Understanding and adapting to those differences is not only important with regards to planning any initiative, but is also crucial in recruiting and retaining the best talent necessary to accomplish those objectives. Whereas senior managers may log off their computers when they leave the office for the day, younger leaders are constantly connected as this connectivity is totally integrated with work, recreation and lifestyle. Social media is not only a preferred communication method but has also become a significant marketing opportunity. As we see the prospect of a global economy becoming a reality, recognizing and being considerate of cultural differences is foundational to both a successful multi-national enterprise and local businesses. This is not only a marketing concern, but a significant Human Resource issue as well because our workforce continues to become more diverse assimilating talent from all nationalities and cultures. I have personally had to mediate situations where employees registered complaints regarding the actions of others who were unaware or insensitive to the cultural norms of a different nationality. Seemingly harmless comments or actions can be very offensive and can only be corrected through awareness and consideration. Left unaddressed, these situations can foster an atmosphere of suspicion and distrust.

Beyond the people aspect of our changing world we are experiencing profound environmental challenges regarding, but not limited to, our carbon footprint, global warming, energy, and fresh water. Legislative attempts to deal with these issues can have a devastating effect on a business heavily invested in processes or products that fall out of favor as a result of the subsequent laws or tax structure. If leaders refuse to recognize the changing dynamic in either their own business or in that of key partners or suppliers, they risk significant loss and displacement as the industry adapts without them. We are also experiencing technological change at such a rapid pace that it is almost impossible to keep up. Businesses with self-designed legacy systems are finding themselves locked into inefficient processes and procedures that are labor intensive and less responsive to user expectations. To remain competitive new technology must be introduced, but the obstacles are great as they deal with sunk costs, personal investment in their present system, and the myopic viewpoints of current users. Our employees trust management to remain abreast of these challenges and make well-timed corrections before the organization falls too far behind to catch up.

As if all of this is not enough, we have not yet touched on actual industry changes. A successful manager must certainly remain abreast of current shifts in their core business groups along with an unobstructed view of the horizon. But in the word of a past co-worker, "It is very clear where we have to go, but we have to find a way to survive until we get there." Yes, it is important to have the correct strategic perspective, but one must also take care of the here and now. Production capabilities, product quality, supply chain optimization, competitive pricing models, and customer relationship management are all minimum requirements for the successful business and the effective manager. To focus too heavily on any one aspect at the expense of the other is risky at best. A leader secure enough to seek out the opinions and expertise of others will be less likely to overlook key aspects that will influence the outcome of the plan and will at the same time strengthen the relationship with staff members.

Craft a strategic course of action:

Even for a small or medium size business, betting on the wrong horse can be, at the very least, a costly error or potentially a knockout punch. Most high dollar capital projects take at least a year and usually a few years to bring to fruition. Planning, engineering, permitting, and construction can take so long that it is very probable that the preferred business model for your endeavor has changed substantially before your project is even completed. Attempts to position yourself in the expected growth area places you on the side of town opposite to where the growth actually occurs or, even worse, you are the last major investor in a business that has suddenly become obsolete. Yet as difficult as the challenge of strategic planning appears to be, it is essential to the longevity and continuity of the business. The only possible hope of success, with the exception of blind luck, is a well thought out plan devised by informed management. Every stakeholder in the business depends on the outcome - from investors, to suppliers, to each of your employees; they have placed their trust in management and it is your responsibility to live up to that trust.

Unfortunately, there are those that spend so much time on strategy that they let the boring day-to-day stuff suffer. Strategic planning is exciting, we get to think outside the box, bring all of our creativity to bear, but current operational data is systematic, familiar, and relentless. There is an old saying that "one can keep their head so high in the clouds that they can't keep their feet on the ground". We truly need a balance between the two even though most of us are better at one than the other. Whereas a major project can deliver a knockout punch in one fell swoop, failing to pay attention to the day-to-day details will just slowly but surely undermine your business with jabs. There are few things so demoralizing than to have worked hard all year, watched enthusiastically as sales grew beyond expectations only to see it all disintegrate like a mirage as unattended-to details erode the company's profitability. Many, if not most, companies perform periodic internal audits designed to uncover these seemingly small deficiencies and managers typically bemoan the exercise. It is import to remember, however, that if these audits are conducted for the right reasons and in a spirit of improvement rather than one of disciplinary action, they are invaluable as a means of protecting earnings from being cannibalized by minor errors or, unfortunately, occasional fraudulent activity.

If managers are to be successful in strategic planning they must constantly re-evaluate their strengths and weaknesses and staff to their limitations. The ultimate test of good management is the performance of the entire team, not just the track record of one stand out manager, employee or department. Additionally, when supervisors, or any of us for that matter, fail to spend adequate time doing what we are good at we tend to lose a sense of enjoyment for the job and experience a diminishing of our energies and creative instincts. If one spends an inordinate amount of time doing only those things that are drudgery, even when they are extremely important to group results and must be done, it is possible to lose sight of why the job was so appealing in the first place. There is no question that these tasks must be accomplished, I only suggest that a person requires a reasonable amount of time involved in those things that interest them in order to re-charge their batteries and maintain their enthusiasm. If that is to happen we must structure our team in such a way that each area is being covered by a person who is not only talented in that aspect of the business, but passionate about it as well. At times this means employing individuals who are actually more talented than we are. Surrounding oneself with the finest talent available that compliments the rest of the team is step one. To quote one of my favorite dramatic lines, delivered by Coach Herb Brooks in the movie "Miracle "(2004, Walt Disney Pictures) that tells the story of the successful 1980 U.S. Olympic Men's Hockey Team, – "I'm not looking for the best players; I'm looking for the right ones." It is how the group performs together that matters, not the individual stats that count. Furthermore, the ability to refrain from feeling threatened by the success of others or worrying about who gets the credit is step two. All too often managers are more worried about how they look or how their individual area of responsibility performs rather than what is the right thing to do for the entire organization.

Provide for its implementation:

One thing I have noticed, over the years, is that a mediocre plan well executed will outperform even the best of plans tardily rolled out or haphazardly put into action. We can spend so much time attempting to craft the perfect strategy that we miss the opportunity altogether. More importantly, however, we often fail to take the correct steps to give the final plan a reasonable probability of success. These steps include insuring that you have the right people in place, communicating effectively, having measurable goals, follow-up on performance expectations, celebrating successes, and refining the plan throughout the process.

If there is one trait most common to successful managers, it is the ability to identify talent. Much like a coach on a winning team, the successful leader has recruited, trained, positioned, and motivated those individuals that bring the necessary aptitudes and attitudes to the workplace. This applies to all classifications and levels of jobs throughout the organization, not just senior positions or supervisors. Even seasoned managers can be surprised by how costly it is to have poor performers even in less critical positions. Unfortunately, even the best of talent can generate lackluster performance if they do not understand the overall plan. Too often supervisors like to dole out information on a "need to know" basis thereby remaining in control, recognizing that knowledge is power. For those of you who are sports fans (in particular football), have you ever noticed how a player can thrive under one coaching system and flounder in another? Or even in a business setting, it is not uncommon to have one departments reject become an outstanding performer in another. I seriously doubt that this individual suddenly improved their skill level, rather I am quite sure the first group did not provide an atmosphere in which those talents could be nurtured and utilized. Good talent needs the right direction to maximize their efforts and that comes from good communication. Excuse me for using an old computer axiom but, "garbage in – garbage out".

Even the most talented individuals can't get the job done if they don't have the necessary tools. Much like government when they pass an unfunded mandate, if we challenge our staff to implement a plan and hold them accountable for results without giving them the necessary tools to accomplish the task; we are only deluding ourselves. Most of us during various periods of our careers have worked under the mantra of "do more with less" and, quite frankly, it does tend to bring out the resourcefulness of the group. But a team must have at least a fighting chance and that only happens when the have access to the necessary resources. Frequently, while still in the planning stage, managers get sidetracked when presenting their concept for approval of either a senior manager or fixed asset committee. As they prepare performance projections that will support their proposed initiative, there is a tendency to overoptimistically tweak the operational models to reach the corporate threshold hurdle rates by skimping on various expense items such as manpower or capital improvements. This may result in a project getting approved, but unfortunately, will lead to unrealistic expectations during the implementation phase. Not just because the original budget for the project should be seen as a commitment, but because in business – if it is in a spreadsheet, it must be correct; regardless of the validity of the underlying data. Nothing will demoralize a group more than leading them on a mission for which they know they are ill-equipped.

Real trust (and performance), however, comes from the hard and often less glamorous work of setting appropriate goals, communicating them effectively and monitoring their progress and, let me firmly stress, in context to ever changing circumstances. I have noticed over the years that many supervisors tend to go for the low hanging fruit, those goals that are easy and quick to measure. I can assure you that there will never be enough time to do all the things demanded of you and, quite frankly, the tendency is to spend more time on what your supervisor has requested of you than the needs of your subordinates or the broader organizational goals. The truth is, nonetheless, that this is a counterproductive approach because superior results don't come from pleasing the "boss" they come from leading your team to success (of course, try not to get fired in the process). The development of meaningful goals that are established through a mutual understanding of the overall objectives of not only your unit, but how they support the rest of the organization will help to create a sense of ownership on the part of the employee. Measuring empirical data is more clear-cut and frequently easier, but can often be misleading; whereas communicating concepts and vision in understandable ways will deliver better results even if ongoing performance is more of a challenge to evaluate. Remember, there is a difference between an excuse and an explanation.

At the end of the day, however, we are all accountable for our performance and contribution to the organization's success requiring us to measure the achievement of the assigned goals. As leaders, our primary assignment is to engage the cooperation of others to achieve those goals and an important tool in making that happen is the periodic review of individual performance on the part of team members. How we handle this review is critical to the long-term relationship, growth and success of the employee. If the goals have been set appropriately as stated above, then taking the time to understand all the relevant data impacting their achievement, we can give honest feedback using the review as a teachable moment rather than a time for criticism. I happen to be one of those odd ducks that enjoyed doing performance appraisals. Not that they were easy to do, mind you, but because it validated and clarified the many spontaneous conversations held previously. It was that time when an employee was encouraged to be open and frank, where they could call me a "no good sob" and at the end of the session we would be on the same page, could shake hands and move on. Additionally, recognizing successes in a sincere way is important. Certainly it makes sense in an appraisal but is even more valuable if these achievements can be recognized in public without causing resentment among the rest of the team.

Champion the effort:

In my office I have a picture of a lighthouse. I don't claim to be a seaman, but I do love the seaside and have always been intrigued by lighthouses and what they are intended to do; be a guiding light, to protect from danger, and be a source of security. As managers, we are called to guide our team toward an objective, we are expected to protect them – keep them out of the ditches so-to-speak, and to give them the security or comfort of knowing that their individual efforts contribute to the larger strategy and that they are not alone in their efforts. All too often, good ideas fail because there is no champion to lead the cause; if you can't get excited about the goal, how can you expect your team to be? The best leaders are the personification of the end results they seek, a focal point that directs the entire team toward that goal and a tenacious advocate of the necessity of their objectives. There is a school of thought that suggests all major projects, if they are to gain traction within the organization, must be sponsored by someone in a C-Level position because that is the only way to achieve cross-divisional buy-in. Individual employees can feel powerless when it comes to negotiating the complex world of organizational politics, but managers who have developed relationships with more senior company officials in various departments and have done their homework with regards to the big-picture implications of their project stand a very good chance of making something happen as well as the clout to have the backs of staff members when things get tough.

One word of caution, don't lead your team on some quixotic mission without getting buy-in from those you report to, it can undermine all of your efforts and the respect of your group. One of the most resilient executives I ever worded for had a way of never taking a position on anything, seemingly believing that if he didn't back any of the horses in the race he would never have to explain a loser. He had the uncanny ability of allowing a subordinate to run an idea up the flagpole to the Chief Operating Officer and evaluate his response before either denying knowledge of the idea or taking credit for sending his subordinate to him with the information. Unfortunately, the messenger loses out either way. For managers to make any headway driving forward good projects it takes a little preliminary work, but can pay off in big ways. Sometimes it takes a longer than we would like, but planting the seeds of an idea enables others to come to the desired way of thinking on their own. To repeat a phrase I have related to some co-workers over the years, "I love it when people come up with my ideas". This usually requires one to put their ego on hold as you let someone else take credit for the idea regardless of whether it is your superior or a staff member, but more importantly, the team wins. Then, as the new idea takes shape and moves forward, it is critical that you as manager provide the necessary backing and support.

Recognize the contribution of others:

When I was a boy of about six or seven, I can still remember how my Mom, after she had spent a great deal of time organizing the kitchen cabinets, would have to show my brother and me her handiwork. As soon as we would come in from playing in the yard, she would begin, with great pride, to open cabinets and slide out drawers displaying how neat, tidy and organized everything was. Naturally, this was completely lost on boys of our age (though I guess not completely lost, as I am remembering it now and yes, my own cabinets are organized), but it demonstrates how eager we all are to have others recognize and appreciate the things we do. Most of us are keenly focused on the things we accomplish and how they contribute to the group effort and, at times, have an exaggerated perception of their importance. Furthermore, when we have a novel or particularly innovative idea, we think the world should stop and take notice. Is it any wonder that staff members should want to be recognized for their labors?

Business is a team effort; it requires the skill and contribution of any number of people who are willing to work toward a common goal. The sales group may have come up with a wonderful growth idea that will need some preliminary investment to accomplish, but the Legal Department must first determine if there are any contractual issues, the Finance team needs to generate predictive models of revenue streams, the Fixed Asset Committee has to appropriate the funds, Logistics will coordinate the arrival of product at the appropriate time for the sales initiative, Operations must insure that the plan is implemented properly and then Marketing must develop a plan to reach the targeted market segment. This does not even take into consideration all of the ancillary services necessary such as Human Recourses, Insurance, Safety, Accounting or IT. Some of you have already experienced the demoralizing effect of a manager taking all of the credit and neglecting to acknowledge the hard work and talent of the rest of the team. The best rule of thumb is to give the team credit for success and you take the blame for failure, it may sting a little but when the chips are down you will have developed a team you can count on because they know they can count on you.

Why is management important? Because if all of the things previously mentioned are done well, not only do we experience a greater probability of business success, but we provide secure and enriching places of employment. Naive as that may sound, organizations of all kinds flourish under this win-win proposition and deteriorate as soon as they begin to cave to the demands of short-term outcomes and overly influenced by segmented data taken out of context to the overall results and objectives of the company. There will always be a need for the abilities of capable managers that can interpret the desires of owners and investors, evaluate the occupational landscape, disseminate information effectively up and down the organizational chain, craft workable tactics and gain the cooperation of others in pursuit of those goals. But, as with most things of importance, this comes at a price – we can't blindly go on our merry way assuming things will be well just because we wish them so.

Pollyanna Doesn't Live Here Anymore

A favorite old Disney movie of mine is the 1960 adaptation of Pollyanna. For those of you who are unfamiliar with the story, Pollyanna was a young lady who lost her missionary parents and came to live with an Aunt (her only living relative) who was a wealthy, Victorian era spinster who dominated the local town activities. Through every trial and tribulation Pollyanna managed to maintain an upbeat and positive outlook by playing what she called the "glad game". She found a way to see something good in every situation, for instance – if someone was picking on her she could be glad because that meant that they were not picking on someone else. Although I have a tendency to be this way myself, it is important to realize that a cheery attitude and good intentions are not all that is necessary to succeed and that there are those who will intentionally do you harm if they feel it will further their own ambitions. This is not intended to scare anyone or create cynicism, just to raise the awareness and generate a healthy dose of reality. Equally as sobering is the fact that we all need to actually have tangible skills. We owe it not just to our employers but to our subordinates as well to refine the abilities necessary to do a good job. This goes for our team members as well. Some of my more regrettable moments have resulted from situations were an individual, by sheer virtue of their engaging personality, ascended to a position for which they were not adequately prepared or failed to keep pace with the changing requirements of the job.

My brother related to me something he had heard a number of years ago that rings true in many situations; "once I accepted the fact that life is hard, it all became so much easier". Similarly, once we accept the fact that our jobs require significant effort, it is much easier to put forth the hard work necessary to become proficient at the requirements of our occupations. It is this willingness to be prepared and to continuously improve that instills confidence in those around you. Just as it is important for you to be the type of person that co-workers can trust, it is equally important to trust others to have the same work ethic, but not blindly.

Why is it important to trust others?

I am a firm believer that if you look for the good in people you will generally find it. Conversely, if you look for the bad you will most likely not be disappointed either. There is a saying coined by The United Methodist Church a few years ago the goes as follows: "*I see you seeing me and I reflect the me I think you see*". Meant to encourage people to be more aware of how our pre-conceived notions of acceptability often send a message to those who may differ significantly from our own norms, this statement suggests that our own attitude tends to reinforce the differences in the other person. I encourage you to re-read the quote (it took me a few times to for it to sink in). Most people tend to respond in ways that correspond very closely to what is expected of them.

Unfortunately, there are managers who look for the bad in others seeming to have the belief that subordinates, or coworkers for that matter, are going to make a mistake (screw up) and they are determined to catch them at it, so the incompetence can be stamped out! Typically using the approach of "shoot first and ask questions latter", they demoralize otherwise well intentioned employees and spawn the very results that they were attempting to eliminate. Even worse for an organization is that the best and the brightest just move on to a company that provides a more productive and nurturing work environment. This can ultimately lead to a downward spiral for the organization as the remaining employees just give in and, more importantly, give up. It is next to impossible to achieve success with an uninspired team.

Far too often, managers will respond to the fist bit of information they receive, lashing out at what appears to be a problem. Phone calls are made and emails are sent, being sure to copy the immediate universe, denouncing such failure. Some of this may even be well intentioned, but for the most part it only serves to act as an opportunity for the manager to enhance their standing among all of those copied and to reinforce their control over the misguided soul who supposedly made the error. The problem is that the first bit of information is generally not accurate or at least not complete, leading one to make assumptions that are not necessarily on target. Years of handling complaints has taught me that no matter how clear-cut the first version of a story appears, there is always another side.

Complicating things even more is our overwhelming tendency to automatically accept computer generated data as fact. I have found it wise to validate unfavorable data before confronting an employee because simple calculation errors can make a huge difference. An accidently changed formula in a spreadsheet, a pointer comparing current results to the wrong time-slice or a failure to poll the most recent daily activity can all make it appear that something is amiss, when in fact it is not. Once the wrong assumption has been jumped to and the employee has been confronted, it is almost impossible to undo the harm once the correct information is brought to light. The resentment, hurt feelings and the wasted time gathering data to support their rebuttal all undermine a healthy trusting relationship.

It has been my experience that most people truly want to give their best, to feel a sense of accomplishment in what they do. The problem, in most cases, is they have misconceptions as to what constitutes a "good job". All too often managers deliver a punch list of things to do without giving the rationale behind them, neglecting a fundamental tenant of organizational dynamics; that people tend to support that which they help to create. If you give the people doing the job some insight as to the overall objectives and allow them some input regarding the best ways to accomplish them, they are more likely to support the necessary changes. (After all, they are already doing the job – shouldn't they know a bit more about that task and how to improve it than an executive who, at best hasn't done it in years, if ever.) More times than not they will come up with better ways to accomplish the stated objectives, if we are open-minded enough to take their suggestions seriously.

Notice, however, that I said most people. One cannot be so naive as to think that there will never be individuals who will disappoint you or worse, but it is important to not let those instances overshadow the real benefits of trusting in others. To be jaded by the few non-performers is no more the right thing to do than to stop giving to charity because there are a few abusers. Spending one's time being overbearing and suspicious of everyone is non-productive and nerve-racking. Frequently, group non-performance is the result of poor communication. When we help employees understand what doing a "good job" really means and how that contributes to the overall objectives of the organization they typically respond in very positive ways, and not just when their supervisor is looking.

Why is it important that others trust you?

There is one concept that over the years I have become more and more certain about; the greatest influence on an employee's job satisfaction is their immediate supervisor. Our business schools are fixated on producing Fortune 500 C.E.O.'s but woefully lacking in preparing students to assume the role of managing individuals. If you want to see how that is done properly, one would only have to go to any Athletic Department where coaches motivate their teams to accomplish sometimes seemingly impossible tasks, all for the sake of the squad. Do coaches always tell a team what they want to hear? – No. Do they insist that each member work their hardest? – Absolutely. What then is the difference? I suggest to you that it is trust, players may not always agree with the coaches' methods or completely understand their actions, but the successful teams trust the coach – they trust him or her because they have earned it.

Isn't it the same in any business or organization? The successful firms are staffed with individuals who are willing to give their best, in great part, because they have supervisors they can trust, manager's they are willing to follow because they have demonstrated a willingness to share the background information, communicate the overriding goals and objectives, clear away obstacles, and then trust them to do their jobs. Does this eliminate the need for follow-up or measuring results; of course not, but in an atmosphere of trust team members can work on correction of errors in a positive fashion producing a setting of continuous improvement. When your team members lack trust in you, they are cautious – unwilling to risk sharing their best ideas or relating the biggest concerns of the group. Both instances can be very costly in either missed opportunities by not taking advantage of an excellent idea or by running into a ditch that could have been avoided if earlier concerns had been voiced.

Although the term Pollyannaish is generally accepted to be overly naive, I can't help but think that (much like in the movie) a healthy dose of that attitude wouldn't be good for us all. Yes, there will be times when looking for the good in others will leave us scratching our heads or making us look foolish, but more often than not our trusting attitude will pay big results as team members give more than they thought they had in them to make the group successful. It won't be during those times of relative success, when everyone is doing well and it appears that all you need to do to succeed is to show up; it will be at those moments when it appears that you are on the brink of failure, those frightening periods when only a herculean effort will do. Those are the times when a team cultivated in such an atmosphere of trust and respect will exceed even our wildest expectations.

Help others look good until they get good:

One of my first jobs, after being self-employed for about ten years was in sales and my assigned area was comprised of multiple retail sites each run by a different manager. Due to an unforeseen departure of one of the location managers, a fairly new management trainee was promoted to the position. True, this individual had great potential, but there was no getting around the fact that he was extremely inexperienced and this was obvious to many of the more tenured employees that he would supervise. Some of these employees would confide in me because we had built up a relationship even prior to my employment in the sales position and the fact that my position did not report to the location managers but, instead, to the Regional Sales Manager. What I told them, and something that has stuck with me over the years, is that we had to make him look good until he got good. There was no question that this individual would develop into a first class manager, but that would not happen if we allowed him to crash and burn on his first assignment. Additionally, what most of us fail to realize is that, the success of the organizations we work for reflects on us as well as the company.

Think for a moment about some ball teams that you have followed, if the team is really bad, do you typically single out certain players and say they are terrific, but the team stinks? I suspect that is not the case and that if the team is thought to be bad, the players are thought of in the same light. By allowing a manager, or any other team member for that matter, to look bad we stand the real chance of allowing the performance of the entire group to suffer. Our customers are not going to listen to you blame shortfalls on the rookie manager and just think that you alone are a great person. They will only see excuses for why things are not going the way they should. When we take the high road and deflect those criticisms rather than allow them to fall squarely on any particular individual, we in many ways defuse the impact of the complaint by spreading the culpability across the entire group. Additionally, we demonstrate our ability to place the group objectives ahead of our own. Rather than attempting to make ourselves look good by distancing our performance from the mistakes of a co-worker, we demonstrate the willingness to accept responsibility and hold ourselves accountable for the actions of the team. Nothing builds trust and cohesiveness within a group more than the confidence that fellow team members have your back.

Believe me, I am not talking about blind trust here or advocating covering for a lack of competency over an indefinite period of time. But, when the new person is working hard and truly means well, it is of no benefit to anyone to let them be the target for excessive criticism. On the other hand, what about when the new person supposedly has the experience and is obviously only concerned with their own itinerary, not the least concerned with the input of the rest of the group? Although this is a much tougher situation to deal with, even in this case it is counterproductive to complain to outsiders such as customers or vendors. When you are faced with internal or external complaints regarding the leader of your team you may need a confidant in a position of influence. I strongly urge you to use this option judiciously and only as a measure of last resort, but understand that it can get ugly. If you are forced to take this approach insure that it is communicated in a professional and confidential manor without even a hint of an underlying self-serving agenda. Double check you motives before proceeding; are these concerns truly a detriment to the organization or just contrary to your own opinion? It is also important to remember that sometimes there are strong relationships that you are unaware of and can backfire on you no matter how well intentioned your concerns. Yet, as precarious as this approach may seem, it may well be the most appropriate action to take.

All in all, it is important to keep in mind that we are typically perceived to be only as good as our entire team so anything we do to enhance the image of the group reflects positively on ourselves. Conversely, when we denigrate others within the group we not only make everyone look bad, but typically we make ourselves appear to be even worse as we are thought to be petty and self-absorbed.

Take a good look in the mirror:

I have on numerous occasions, over the years, had to take a step back and truly re-evaluate my circumstances, am I heading in the direction that I intended to go and if not what changes I might need to make to get back on course, even occasionally consider an entirely new direction. This process of self-evaluation is not always pleasant because I typically uncover weakness within myself that I have attempted to conceal or just not acknowledge. The fact of the matter is, however, that we so often find ourselves traveling on the path of least resistance and find ourselves a tad bit off course. It seems to be a very human tendency to place the blame for these detours on fate, circumstance or other people, when quite frankly it is usually our unwillingness to face the things that must be done to make the correction. For me, taking a good look in the mirror is more than just a figure of speech, it is actually when I have generally come to these realizations. Of-times this epiphany presents itself while shaving in the morning; while looking at myself in the mirror the culmination of weeks of thought and contemplation come crashing in presenting the only tenable scenario – I need to make a change. Sometimes this change can be as simple as deciding to improve my attitude, to approach my current activities with a renewed vigor. There are other times, however, when that decision involves a much lengthier commitment such as deciding to seek additional education or change careers.

Nevertheless, whether your awakening comes while actually looking in the mirror or just doing so figuratively, it is imperative that each of us routinely evaluate not only our individual goals, but our effectiveness in doing the varied tasks that we are expected to accomplish. Before complaining about the shortcomings of others, be sure to take a close look at your own performance and contribution. The Bible saying "Let he who is without sin cast the first stone" (John 8:7) works pretty well in a business environment where we are all too eager to point the finger at someone else. Are there times when we may well be the obstacle to optimum performance? In one management assignment, I found that things were not getting done in a timely fashion. My first inclination was to blame the individuals responsible for completing the work, but upon further reflection, I came to the conclusion that the reason they weren't getting things done on time was that they were getting their orders late. Why? Because I insisted that each order be reviewed by me first, not willing to trust others to get it right. I was the bottleneck! These were very competent people and once I took the time to train them and then trusted them to handle the process on their own, the problem went away and everything operated much more efficiently.

We have all heard or been involved in peer evaluations or 360° reviews, each of which are intended to give us a better perspective on how effective we are and help us be more aware of our potential blind spots, but nothing can be more effective than a good honest look at ourselves and be willing to make the necessary adjustments.

Demonstrating Trust in People

Of course, accepting the altruistic goal of trusting people, as the saying goes; talks easy and works hard. One lesson I learned very early in my career was that not everyone does things the same way I would do them, but that does not mean that their method was not equally as good (if not better) than mine. Additionally, we will all make a wrong call from time to time causing us to second guess our abilities or even our seasoned intuitive response to various situations. It is our responsibility as managers to create a nurturing environment where staff members feel secure in making the right choices when called upon to do so. Proponents of centralized management feel that if you have enough corporate oversight and minutely detailed policies and procedures every situation can be carefully scripted. It has been my experience however, that the workplace is not that neat and tidy. Employees need to be educated and empowered so they are more likely to make decisions similar to what senior management would do in the same circumstance. The following points are ways in which one can begin to create the kind of workplace where individuals make the best decisions.

Clearing away the obstacles:

Executive teams love neat and tidy numbers, roll-ups that give them a quick overview of what is going on in the organization. For the most part this is a good and necessary capability enabling a relatively few people who control the purse strings and overall direction of the company to make accurate decisions. The most current management information systems utilize dashboards to present key informational, statistical and operational data in systematic and organized fashion in order that more accurate and timely decisions can be made. All too often, the generalizations made from aggregate results paint a picture that is misleading, very much like the non-existent sku in statistics (for example; the family with 2.5 children). Only by drilling down to the underlying data can one target the true area that needs attention, but the tendency is to give blanket direction to the entire group thereby actually hurting those that have actually been performing well. To coin a phrase I have picked up over the years, "no good deed goes unpunished". We have an affinity for looking at the aggregated data and assuming that it applies equally across all segments.

One instance in particular stands out regarding a particular business unit I was responsible for. This facility had one main location and two branch operations all rolling up to a single operating statement. The business had been delivering less than adequate results for a few years prior to my assuming this operation as part of my unit. Previously all attempts to correct the poor results had been directed at the entire operation and even included changing General Managers more than once, unfortunately the real issues were decisions that needed to be made above the General Manager's control. The real problems resided in the branch operations that were being camouflaged by the performance of the main location. Previous evaluations had relied entirely on the aggregate data thereby masking the key issues needing attention. By clearing away the debris (selling one branch and renting out the other) we enabled the local manager to operate his business profitably and generate consistently better than average results in both earnings and return on capital. When he did not have to spend so much time evaluating the problems caused by the branch facilities, he was able to focus on growing his core business profitably. Those with the authority to correct the problem were also the farthest away from the day-to-day operations and heavily influenced by the composite financial results, thus leaving the local General Manager helpless to effect the necessary changes. Once those changes were made the situation improved dramatically.

Sometimes clearing away obstacles can mean addressing a personal limitation on the part of the employee; off-times this is a training issue or a gap in education. We do a terrible disservice to quality staff members if we ignore, or worse, compensate them for the lack of necessary capabilities. Much like passing an elementary student before they actually master the needed skills will set them up for future failure, we can also allow a quality employee to feel an unwarranted sense of security when in fact they lack the foundational resources to succeed in the future. A prime example of this is a long tenured staff member that still has 15 or 20 years to work but has fallen woefully behind on current business technology. Not only will it hurt their performance and chances for promotion within the organization, but if for some reason they needed to replace their current job in the workplace they would not have the skills necessary to compete with other applicants. It is situations like this that require us to use our coaching skills to create awareness within the individual of the weakness without damaging their self-esteem and providing possible educational solutions. The reality is that they were good enough to get where they are today, that same ability to succeed will be an asset in the future with a little training. If we were talking about marketing a product we would call this extending the product life-cycle, if we refer to this as the employee life-cycle (for, in fact, we all behave in this manor to some extent) providing for this extended period of peak productivity is mutually beneficial to the individual and the organization.

Of course, neither altering the complexity of an operation nor changing a person's attitude is always easy or successful. People are personally invested in what they do and how they do it, frequently because they may have been doing it a certain way for a lengthy period of time. One must attempt to first understand the situation and the rationale behind their current decision process. I will always remember a large sign hanging in the service bay at an automobile dealer I used a number of years ago; it stated "Beware of the mechanic who has the answer to your problem before he has even listened to what the trouble is." We must be careful about our pre-conceived ideas, there may be perfectly logical reasons for why things are the way they are and may well change our opinion of how to make them better. But, in the end, we must take action and not be stymied by a lack of all-conclusive data. Some individuals are open to logical discussion others, unfortunately, need a "wake-up call". As much as I dislike creating stress for an individual, at least in one instance it was the best thing to do for the person. I actually had to ask the individual (a manager I greatly respected) how many years he planned to work until he retired. He responded "ten or twelve more years" to which I replied with another question, "what if your business is only going to last five more years?" He was noticeably shaken because he had never considered that possibility, but the fact was unless some change in course took place that is exactly what would happen. Fortunately, he made the necessary changes and they proved to be both profitable and personally rewarding for him. He even had to admit that he should have made the changes earlier. Even when the course of action is difficult, I am a firm believer that if you do the right things for the right reasons, eventually you will achieve the right outcomes.

Confide in your employees – share the data:

For some time social thinkers such as Alvin Toffler and business gurus like the late Peter Drucker have expressed the critical part information plays in today's economy and that having and controlling information is power. There is absolutely no question that accurate and appropriate data improves decision making in any organization. However, much like how a personality test will identify a valued quality in an individual that, taken to the extreme, can have a flip side that is detrimental. (Honesty is a valued trait – being so honest that I tell you your shirt sucks and you need to lose 10 pounds - maybe not so much)

The concept of information as power can be taken to extremes where staff is informed on a *need to know* basis – "I am important because I know and you don't". The reality is that the more thoroughly and efficiently good information is disseminated throughout an organization the greater the actual performance and, ironically, the better the particular supervisor or senior staff looks in the eyes of their superiors and peers alike. All too often leaders in a company have the exaggerated opinion of self-worth that they believe they are the only ones capable of evaluating the data and making informed decisions. The problem is that they are usually so removed from the actual source of that data that they can't recognize obvious anomalies and when front-line people try to explain the information leaders tend to view their input as excuses rather than an attempt to create an accurate picture of the situation.

One of the key requirements in any successful group is to have the best and most capable individuals at the "frontline" where we interact with customers, generate revenue, build relationships with clients, or manufacture a product. No amount of top-down management can compensate for second best choices at these positions. Yes, we can help them see the "big picture" and counsel them with regards to possible blind spots, but in the end we must trust them to make good decisions, decisions that are best when influenced by accurate and timely data. By providing information in efficient and usable formats we enhance their ability to recognize when something is amiss and take corrective action much sooner than would be if we wait for some staff business analyst to generate a report that is filtered down through someone's boss's boss. By the time information circles back through all of those layers of management and back to the front-line, the battle has probably already been lost.

The real challenge is how do we attract and retain the top quality people needed in these positions. It is my opinion that we only do this by continually raising the bar and encouraging people to expand their knowledge base and skill set. Unfortunately there is a tendency in many organizations to "dumb-down" frontline managers by centralized administrative approaches and punch list directives that squash the entrepreneurial spirit of the brightest and the best. There is no question that maintaining quality management at ground-zero is a daunting task. Not only must an organization compete with other companies seeking similarly talented individuals, but the best and the brightest will always have opportunities to move up within your own firm resulting in constant churn at these critical positions. Only by providing them with the best information, encouraging continued learning, and providing insight to the larger organizational needs can we develop truly successful managers for today and exceptional leaders for tomorrow.

Creating the right expectations:

I firmly believe that the majority of people want to do a good job, to make a difference, and be successful. All too often they can be hampered by what I will term a *misguided work ethic*. Employees will sincerely attempt to do that which they think to be of benefit for the institution in any given situation. Unfortunately, they do not always have a clear picture of what is truly best or even acceptable because no one has communicated the complete objective or why it is important, which may not be obvious to the employee at that time. Frequently this happens when we fail to recognize the fact that our staff members will try to respond to even our most carelessly made comments as well as model our own behavior.

If you don't think that your staff attempts to model your behavior, come in in a bad mood one day and observe what it does to the entire team. How a manager conducts themselves sets the tone for their entire group and ironically, some of a manager's best qualities can backfire in terms of individual performance. One obvious action, yet often overlooked is the number of hours you spend on the job. Being willing to put in the necessary time and working until the job is done is not only commendable, but mandatory if one is to be a successful leader. I doubt seriously if managers at any level can get by with less than 50 to 60 hours a week and some go far beyond that. If the employee attempting to model your behavior is paid hourly and overtime is a serious concern at your company, there is an obvious rub. The employee equates doing a good job with working the hours equivalent to what they see you doing. After many years in operations, I can say with great confidence that 10 to 20 hours of overtime for each employee can destroy a unit's payroll budget. Does this mean that a manager needs to curtail the amount of time they put in? Probably not, but It does mean that there needs to be clear and open communication with the group as to the overriding needs of the business as well as the expectations of the manager. Our responsibility is to help employees understand what actions are truly beneficial to the organization.

At times our requests or even just offhanded comments can set in motion a chain reaction of events that are unproductive and, on occasion, disruptive. The old saying "be careful what you ask for" certainly applies in these situations. Managers often fail to recognize the potential implications of requesting and measuring the wrong information. Even seemingly meaningless inquiries or comments can set off an unintended chain of events that divert employee attention from the real goals and objectives or even worse, set them on a course opposite to the one envisioned. If a supervisor always reviews certain bits of information regarding a particular division or business unit, the staff in that unit will naturally begin to take steps to improve the factors that contribute to that data. The rationale being, "if the boss thinks it is important – it must be" even if it means wasting precious time on something that is immaterial to actual performance. Senior Managers must be very careful of this pitfall because they can instigate a wild goose chase throughout an entire organization as mid-level managers attempt to curry favor and eventual promotions.

The hidden jewel in all of this is that people will, in fact, respond to those things a supervisor pays attention to; hence the business axiom "inspect what you expect". If one will consistently review those things that drive performance (the importance of measuring those accurately will be addressed in the next section) an unspoken message is sent as to where team members should focus their attention. The trick of course is to insure that what is being reviewed is focused on the right things. The question then becomes; how do we send the right message? I suggest that it begins by having a foundational understanding of the inner workings of the particular operational unit and how that unit contributes to the overall objectives of the entire organization. This may be a tall order, given that many companies will recruit leaders from non-related businesses to bring in a fresh approach, and although this can be beneficial in some ways, it can create confusion and inefficiencies as they ask the wrong questions, or do things at the wrong time in an attempt to make a difference in their new position. Few companies (or results oriented individuals for that matter) are willing to take the time to fully comprehend the way all of the pieces of the puzzle fit, yet when that leader has a comprehensive perspective of the company the results can be impressive as they were with one particular leader I have worked with.

Agricultural Cooperatives can be very complicated entities both in the varied businesses in which they participate and in what constitutes success in the eyes of their owners. Without going into great detail, cooperatives are owned and operated by and for the benefit of their users. In the case of a farmer owned cooperative, the farmers that use it (typically the largest customer segment) are the owners of the corporation. These companies can be involved in traditional in-store retail sales, commercial manufacturing of Feed and Fertilizers, distributors of farm related chemicals, and the procurement and distribution of Petroleum Products. Each of these segments has their own industry idiosyncrasies that are frequently misunderstood by the others. I had the pleasure of observing one particular Chief Operating Officer who ran the business with the fluidity of an orchestra's conductor. Because he had spent years in various parts of the business, he was able to fully comprehend how all the pieces fit. His familiarity with each of the business segments enabled him to glean information from operational reports and understand what needed tweaking and what should be left alone without sending armies of business analysts in search of data (which typically requires front line people to stop what they are doing and collect and report information). Granted, a company does not always have the luxury of having such experience at the helm, but the closer to it we get, the better it is for the organization. This C.O.O. was able to trust key employees throughout the organization because, one – he was familiar enough with the inner-workings of the company to spot a snow job a mile away and two – everyone knew that he knew.

Giving a clear sense of what is most important to all employees is essential to success, but sending mixed messages as to what those things are is frustrating and counterproductive. There is an old saying "if everything is an emergency, nothing is an emergency"; I believe it could be rephrased "if everything is the most important, nothing is most important". By frequently sending staff members on wild goose chases to gather information that proves to be unhelpful, or worse – unnecessary, we send a message of no confidence. We develop an atmosphere of suspicion and second guessing as staff members are constantly on guard. Even worse is how this type of burdensome oversight reduces productivity because individuals are always second guessing their natural instincts and constantly off-balance never able to settle into a natural creative flow. Have you ever tried to coach a young baseball player on how to improve their batting? You start with a youngster who may have some natural ability to hit the ball, yet we tell them how to improve their stance, to get their feet positioned just right in the batter's box. We then begin to instruct them how to bend their knees just enough to get some spring in their movement, followed by keeping their arms up and bat back. Of course then comes keeping your eye on the ball and having a smooth follow through on the swing. Unfortunately, the very next time they get up to bat they are so confused they are almost awkward because instead of paying attention to the pitcher and swinging instinctively they are re-playing your instructions over and over in their head. This is the very same affect we have on our employees when we show a lack of trust because we don't know what we should be looking for.

Measuring performance appropriately:

There is a well-regarded business axiom that states "if you can't measure it you can't manage it" and while I agree with that concept completely, the real fly in the ointment is, so to speak; are we measuring the right things? All too often we are tracking symptoms not causes and making the assumption that a cause and effect relationship exists. Of course discerning the most meaningful data related to any given problem can be challenging, but there is one factor that seems to be most frequently the root cause of discrepancies, the inexperience of the person seeking the information. It is not uncommon for a senior manager, especially in the executive ranks, to wind up in charge of a business unit for which they have no foundational experience. Having never worked in that area of operations there is a tendency to notice that various pieces of performance data move in relationship to each other and consequently, if you drive one it must inevitably move the other. Unfortunately, this is frequently not the case and can lead to poor decisions with regard to staffing and capital expenditures along with frustration on the part of those who actually do know the business because they as they are being measured against ill-conceived benchmarks.

A case in point is a company I am familiar with that was in a few diverse businesses, one of which was Propane. A new executive, who was well versed in many aspects of the other businesses but completely lacking even cursory understanding of this one, decided after reviewing the data that the key to growth was tank sets. By way of background, in the Propane business each customer must have a tank installed that complies with industry and regulatory standards and is often owned and maintained by the supplier. Armed with this informational insight, he proceeded to add additional equipment, manpower, and tank inventory to support the initiative of setting more tanks. The lack of first-hand knowledge of the business and a reluctance to trust the advice of those that had it resulted in a large increase in both fixed and variable expenses that plagued that part of the business for a number of years. New customer growth actually came as a result of a healthy economy, housing starts, demographics and brand awareness – the number of tanks set was a symptom of success not its cause. That does not, however mean that tracking this particular metric is not of benefit, the important thing to remember is that the information must be viewed in context to other influences and whether it is a leading or trailing indicator.

To be fair, evaluating those influences is rather problematic, as it is difficult to discern differences between actual causes or leading indicators and mere symptoms which are trailing indicators. I suggest that we approach the subject from two directions, simulation and causation, beginning with the latter. The real struggle with causes are that they typically cannot be measured until after the event. For instance, one can't measure the impact of a virus until after people get sick and even then, if we are measuring whether or not someone has head congestion, the illness may actually be from a different cause, in this case possibly allergies not a virus. We can use the information after the fact to determine if methods of prevention were better or worse than expected or how things may be improved going forward, but it is of little help determining if you, I or any other individual will get sick the next time. At other times, causes are more elusive or so broad in nature that they are almost impossible to predict. Using the tank example from earlier, a strong economy and increased housing starts are certainly causes for growth, but predicting them accurately is challenging even for some of the world's best economists. Something more readily in the public purview is the weather; the conditions may appear to be right for rain, but one can never be 100% sure, nor are these conditions causes until it actually rains. One thing that most people like about measuring causes is that there is accuracy in the numbers; ten people got the flu therefore ten people were exposed to the virus and so on. Simulations, on the other hand are not so neat and tidy, they assimilate as much relevant data as possible with each set weighted appropriately to its influence on the outcome. Whether done consciously or intuitively, the process provides an approximation of the situation or the resulting outcome.

A good friend of mine who is a very gifted accountant only finds credibility in those reports where everything adds up exactly. In most cases, especially with regards to financial reports, this is an absolute must, but there are times when demanding absolute accuracy may eliminate some very good tools of measurement and forecasting. Case in point; the weather forecast is never completely accurate, yet most - if not all of us, check the forecast before leaving home and take an umbrella when they say it is supposed to rain. More often than not there is significant benefit in using simulation to predict or measure those things that are difficult to quantify even when the numbers don't always add to a perfect sum. More often than not, simulation gives us what I like to refer to as goodness-badness indicators; the ability to keep pointing us in the right general direction even if it is not a perfectly mapped out course. Most of us find comfort in readily comparable data, especially if that data is relatively easy to capture. Consequently, it is not uncommon to go for the low hanging fruit of easily captured and compared figures, even if the information may not give us a true picture of the situation. Of course today we have the enormous benefit of technological advances in artificial intelligence and the use of predictive modeling that enables the use of multiple sources of information and sometimes what might seem like unrelated statistics to demonstrate the correlation between events, but even that does not deliver certainties, just much more refined projections. More often than not, it is the best judgment of those most experienced and closest to the task that, in conjunction with the most accurate data available, actually have the best chance of making good projections. Not to overuse sports analogies, but think if you will of an NFL quarterback. The coaches have developed a game plan using statistical data on the tendencies of the opposing team as well as the strengths of their own. But once in the game, the difference between the average QB and the exceptional ones and usually between winning and losing is the ability of the quarterback to read the defensive formations prior to the snap of the ball and make adjustments in the play called on the spot. How is he able to do that? He can because of his experience, training and natural instincts. Our best frontline people have the same kind of instincts when it comes to the business environment in which they operate; what the competition will do, the external factors that may affect demand and a keen instinct as to how and when they should respond. To remove them from the equation would be much like taking away the ability of a quarterback to call an audible.

We must take advantage of all the data available to us and identify those things that are leading indicators that may be helpful in forecasting and those that are trailing indicators for measurement and evaluation. Then, utilizing the best computing capabilities available to us, suggest possible scenarios, but never rely on data alone, especially in the hands of the inexperienced. When making forward looking decisions or evaluating performance make sure to involve the insight and recommendation of those most familiar with the actual task in question. They will help you refine the process and keep everyone out of the ditches.

The things that one measures actually send a message to the entire staff as to what is considered to be important and those are the things they begin to focus on. The best employees will know that what is being tracked is frequently not in sync with the most important goals, but will still attempt to give management what they have asked for resulting in frustration and, at times, apathy. Of-times their efforts to communicate to management the true impact of the current initiative are perceived as resistance to change or unwillingness to be a team player. Additionally, misguided directives result in the need for increased levels of follow-up and oversight to insure the proper level of compliance within the group. Individuals will do what is necessary to maintain an acceptable performance score, even if that means doing things that are actually at odds with the true intent of the procedures in the first place.

Only by cultivating an atmosphere of trust and participative management can senior administrators improve their chances of focusing on the main things and directing everyone's attention to the key objectives necessary for the success of the organization. This does not mean, however, that one should turn a blind-eye to the need for change and the resistance that often accompanies it. Any number of external and internal developments can necessitate doing things differently and many times it is the senior manager that can have a broader view of their impact, but it is only through the insight of front-line personnel that response to those factors can be truly effective. Change and the importance of communicating the need effectively will be addresses in another section on challenging growth and adopting change.

Give credit where credit is due:

Recognition for a job well done is one of the greatest motivators with regard to performance and self-esteem, yet our tendency as supervisors is to concentrate on negative performance and corrective measures. Far too many managers have the attitude "I know you are going to screw-up and I'm going to catch you at it". Unfortunately, this almost always generates outcomes opposite to those desired. Daniel Goleman in his book "Focus" (Publisher: HarperCollins Publishers, Publication date: 10/8/2013) relates one element of maintaining appropriate focus is through positive, rather than negative, feedback to employees. "Steadfast focus on the negative.....creates a toxic climate that dispirits those they lead. Such leaders may get short term results through personal heroics, like going out and getting a deal themselves, but do so at the expense of building their organizations." Positive comments, on the other hand, tend to keep staff members thoroughly engaged in the task at hand whereas negative feedback results in distraction and poor performance. Additionally, it is human nature to seek positive feedback for our contributions to any endeavor and that certainly holds true for managers at any level. Any supervisor yearns to be recognized for their contribution, yet it is difficult (and actually quite counter-intuitive) not to seek it because they are measured by the performance of their team. Teams perform better when individual team members are given the credit, if a manager does their job well it will appear that they did very little to achieve the successful outcome because the credit went to team members.

The general sentiment goes something like this; "anyone could have done well if they had that team". One can only hope that discerning senior executives recognize the ability of the manager to orchestrate the development and coordination of the team's efforts. It is the track record of the manager, over time, that demonstrates this ability and that takes patience waiting for it to be recognized, a level of patience many are not capable of.

Frustrated and unappreciated employees are focusing their attentions on: Will I lose my job? Should I start sending out my resume? How come they can't see the things I have done well? Or the perceived incompetence of the person being critical will all weigh heavily on the employee who feels marginalized or unappreciated. This is not to say that true deficiencies do not need to be addressed effectively (this will be discussed in the next section) but creating an atmosphere of suspicion and tension is most certainly counterproductive. It has been my experience that the overwhelming majority of employees truly want to do the right things, yet we as managers have not always done a good job of communicating what those right things are.

Think, if you will, of a time when you were complimented for something you had done; didn't it feel wonderful? So much so that one usually tries to recreate that experience by doing something equivalent again and again. Years ago, while coaching a little league football team, I had one young man who was big for his age, although a tad bit awkward. He was not naturally gifted or a particularly good player, but tell him he did a good job on a specific play and he would give you even more the next. I can still see this 10 year old player staring up at me with a bloody mouth from the previous play saying I can do it coach – keep me in. Wouldn't you want your employees saying "I can do it – keep me in!"

Encouraging comments don't just last for the moment, on occasion they last for a lifetime. As a young teen of about 13 or 14, I had been requested to read scripture in front of our congregation one Sunday morning. Of course I was terribly nervous as this was a first for me and at that time adults were the only ones asked to read bible passages in front of the entire church. I was prepared and assume it went reasonably well, but what I remember most was the comment afterwards to me in front of a group of adults by a close friend of my mother who had a year or so earlier been my Sunday School teacher; "If you can do that so well, there is nothing you will not be able to achieve in life if you set your mind to it". Over the years that one comment has come rushing back whenever I faced doubts or challenges. I am sure my mother's friend, who is now deceased, never realized how much that comment meant to me. There are probably countless times we have made comments to others, good or bad, that have stayed with them for long periods of time. Think of the impact you could have if those were comments that motivated them to do bigger and better things.

Acknowledging people's contributions and celebrating their successes not only builds trust but it supercharges their batteries. Feeling that one is appreciated and valued is a very powerful motivator creating the confidence necessary to think out-of-the-box and innovate. Supporting an atmosphere of innovation results in a breeding ground for new ideas – new approaches to old problems – the kind of ideas that differentiate your company from competitors.

Address weaknesses compassionately:

One individual I worked with and for whom I have enormous respect was highly intelligent, successful, competent at his job, and one of the hardest workers I have known. Unfortunately, he has struggled building a strong team because no one ever lived up to his standards. He had a very low tolerance level for anyone who was not as bright as he was, and it was obvious to those around him, therefore short-circuiting opportunities to grow talent, undermining the processes of hiring it and negating the opportunity to build a trusting atmosphere that retained talented individuals. This is not to say that having appropriate skills is unnecessary, quite the contrary. Group performance, however, is determined by the collective skills of any entity and competitive advantage derived from your organization's being greater than another's. There are three crucial focal points that revolve around addressing individual weakness; hiring appropriately, the ability of the individual to develop the necessary skills, and counseling and grooming the individual with regards to their strengths.

Hiring appropriately may seem extremely obvious (duh….), but until one has experienced the ramifications of making the wrong choice it is difficult to fully grasp the need to take your time, evaluate thoroughly, and utilize all the resources available to make the right selection. Of course the pressure is to fill the spot quickly because trying to do your own job as well as the one that is vacant is draining, but not nearly as draining as fixing all of the issues left in the wake of choosing a poorly suited staff member. It is not unusual that a wrong call in a managerial or supervisory position can cost the company in excess of $100,000 through salary, lost productivity of the team, defection of their direct reports to a better place to work, disgruntled customers, lost sales, and the expense of doing it all over again to find the right person.

I once hired a Branch Manager who, at a quick glance, seemed to have the necessary skills to handle the position. His resume looked good, had experience in related jobs but I neglected to spend enough time determining if he was the right fit for the position. As it turned out, his management style was ill-suited for this particular position and he alienated the entire staff, but the biggest issue happened with a customer. First, let me give you a little insight as to the organizational structure as a background for the incident. In this case, a branch location was operationally connected and reported to a larger mother location only fifteen minutes away that had a more extensive product and service offering but both locations shared the same accounts receivables. The branch handled a lot of smaller consumer items whereas the larger location handled mostly high-dollar business-to-business accounts. The single largest account (above six figures annually) at the mother location was on his way home and stopped into the branch location to pick up a small item at the request of his wife. This happened to be during the peak of his busy season and his account was at its highest level of the year. This was not uncommon for the largest accounts and the General Manager had the authority to override or increase the amount when justified. When this prime customer went to check out the $10 item for his wife, he was informed by the Branch Manager that he could not run the charge (the branch manager had visibility to the AR balance). Upon hearing this the customer asked, "You mean I can't charge it?" to which the Branch Manager responded indignantly "don't you think you've charged enough!" The unyielding, everything is black or white attitude of the Branch Manager could have cost the company a very valuable account. Fortunately, this customer had a great sense of humor and we were able to laugh it off, but it was an indication of how poorly suited this individual was for the branch manager position and that changes eventually had to be made.

A poor hiring decision is not just costly for your organization; it is costly to the person hired also. Placing someone in a job that they are not suited for sets them up for failure and keeps them from continuing to search for that "right fit" – the position that will help them grow as an individual and make a positive contribution. I firmly believe that people want to be productive and influence the organization in ways that make it better. To be deprived of that is demoralizing and stressful resulting in numerous challenges from increased negativity, depression, and a potential set-back that some never quite recover from. Taken one step further there are often family consequences as decisions are made and schedules arranged.

A former co-worker of mine was a well-educated and talented individual with a great personality and the ability to build networks of others that would work together in solving problems. Because of his obvious talents he was afforded opportunities to advance in his career, but was hurt immeasurably by an uncaring executive who put him in a position he was not yet prepared for. This co-worker had good financial skills, but had always worked in staff positions never having been involved with operations or supervising people. This particular executive had a track record of putting people in sink-or-swim situations not particularly concerned if he lost a few along the way; after all there are plenty more employees were they came from. This employee was placed in a position where the team he managed had far more operational and supervisory experience than he had and his peers were light-years ahead of him in expertise. The experience resulted in a failure that could have been avoided. A talented individual that could have easily mastered the job (and bigger jobs for that matter) if given a chance to build the necessary foundational skills first was removed from the positon and tagged as a failure. Of course he was not and began the slow process of re-building his career path, but it was a major set-back for him and a huge loss for the company as they were not able to maximize his potential contribution.

Once a person is hired it then becomes imperative that we give them every opportunity to succeed even when that individual may turn out to be lacking in the full array of skills we had hoped for. First and foremost we must determine which of those skills are essential and material to the success of the unit and which are nice to have but not "show-stoppers". Each of us have personal preferences, a tendency to prefer people much like ourselves, but not only can employees vastly different from you perform well, it is actually essential as you attempt to interact with a diverse group of co-workers and clients. The very people who do not relate well to you (yes, believe it or not, not everybody loves you) may relate well to that employee or customer who rubs you the wrong way. Additionally, it is not uncommon for an individual to assimilate with the group norms seeking to fit in, gradually becoming more and more like the rest, but remember – diversity is a good thing!

The real challenge is when a critical skill is not up to the performance standards necessary to do the job at the expected level. This can be a delicate and highly personal situation for both the employee lacking the capabilities and the manager who may well have hired them, as each has their reputation at stake and are personally vested in the outcome. One of the best things managers can do in any issue regarding performance related to individual capabilities is to counsel the employee with regards to the gap between the desired skill set and the observed performance. Here is where the going gets tough. If we are to have any success in fixing the situation, we must keep two objectives firmly planted at the center of our actions; first – the needs of the organization and second – a desire to truly help the employee. There are times when so called counseling sessions are merely perceived as an opportunity to drive home the weaknesses of the employee as a precursor to termination. While there is the reality of our litigious society and the resulting need for documenting poor performance, we are best served by identifying the underlying reasons behind the shortcomings and addressing them in a fashion that delivers the required performance level yet still leaves the employee with a feeling of self-worth and an opportunity to contribute. It is important to ascertain whether the job requirements have changed since the individual was placed in it or did they, for one reason or another, get placed in a job for which they were not completely qualified. Addressing the latter situation first, it goes without saying that if an applicant truly misrepresented themselves there is a clear case for termination. But what if that applicant merely exaggerated their capabilities? Not maliciously, just in an overzealous effort to get the job and they appear to be a good employee otherwise. (As my mother used to say to me when I had taken more of my favorite food than I could possibly eat; "your eyes are too big for your belly".) Anyone who has ever read a few resumes can attest to the fact that many people have a propensity to embellish their qualifications. It may well be in the organization's best interest to make use of this employee's existing talents while they are prepared to handle the questionable tasks at some later date, or is it possible to restructure a couple of positions reassigning the task in question. Either way, by handling the situation in a compassionate manor you may have not only left the employee with their integrity as well as helped them identify a weakness that can be fixed, but you also retained an individual who seemed to be a good fit for the company.

With regards to the situation where the job requirements have changed since the employee took the position, it is important to give them every opportunity to obtain those skills. These are times when it is a training issue, a time when we need to provide avenues for the employee to grow and hone their skills. Remember, training does not only apply to newly hired team members, all too often people of tenure that have contributed much over the years can exhibit signs of falling behind the current expectations of proficiency. When it comes to personnel, it is almost always better to fix than to switch. Frequently we fail to recognize the value of institutional knowledge – the ability to navigate the system, know who to contact to get things done, and the reason we do things the way we do. When someone new comes into a position it can take months to recover the efficiency lost during the transition. Giving people the opportunity to learn, grow, and improve generates loyalty and sends a message to all employees that people are valued.

We have all heard the saying "you can lead a horse to water but you can't make him drink", well that is true with training opportunities. There will be times when an individual is either unable or unwilling to improve through training. Once in a while they will not have the foundational knowledge or experience to move forward (one of the hazards of promoting people too quickly) or far too often because they are too heavily invested in the way things have always been and resist change. In either situation it is important that we have a formal meeting with the employee (this is a more structured and formal meeting than the counseling session mentioned above) where the gap between expectations and performance are clearly articulated with written, goals, timelines, and consequences. This step is dreaded by most of us, but terminating someone should be hard – if it isn't, you are in the wrong job. Don't allow the formality of the meeting to restrict you from being sincere and offering heartfelt recommendations – it is OK to show you care. Done properly, however, it can give the individual a jump-start to make the necessary improvements or the self-realization that they would be happier and more productive moving in another direction. It is critically important that we do not jump to this step before we have exhausted other training and coaching options both for the employee's sake and for your own. You will feel much better about yourself if you are confident you did all you could for the person while doing the right thing for the company at the same time.

Strongly support continuous learning:

Nothing is more upsetting than to have a person working for you who no longer has the skills to compete in the workplace for the very job they already have. Or a 50 year old who still has over 15 years to work, yet are already woefully behind industry changes or technological advances. All too often people have the misguided idea that once they complete their formal education (High School, College, or Graduate Degree) they are done with school. Fortunately, many professions already require continued training through the implementation of C.E.U's that are incorporated as part of their work goals and performance appraisals. These training modules, even though excellent for vocationally specific training, still may leave the individual lacking some components of a well-rounded culturally relevant team member. Just what are the signs of a valued team member falling behind, and how should a supervisor address it?

By way of an example, I had a number of my highest performing managers that fell into this category. This group, in their early 40's, was energetic, experienced, professional, and very successful – they knew how to drive earnings. Common wisdom would say "if it aint broke – don't fix it" why take the chance of upsetting the highest earners in the group. While that is often the best approach, in this case it would have been an injustice to the individuals and, in the long run, not the best thing for the company either. On average they had been out of school almost 20 years (How much has technology changed in the last 10 years, much less 20?), yet most of these managers did not recognize the widening gap developing between their own capabilities and the current broadly accepted technology. Not only were they lacking in the ability to use the newer technologies but they did not recognize how these new tools were fundamentally changing the way business is conducted and how their jobs needed to be performed. And this is not confined to only their own jobs, but to their staff members as well since computerization has removed redundancies, eliminated certain tasks, and fostered mobility. These managers started their career at a time when administrative demands kept them *chained to their desks* scouring hard-copy reports and giving direction to team members. Today those energies should be directed toward being out among clients and employees where the work is actually taking place selling, coaching, connecting with key stakeholders and reviewing data on the fly through the use of various mobile technologies. Many are finding it hard to leave their comfort zone – the way they have always done it - and adjusting to the pace of an always connected environment, but their survival depends on it. And for those of you who are confident that you are already proficient in the current technologies; let me ask you a question – do you honestly think the pace of change will slow down over your next 10, 15, or 20 years?

How then do we approach these situations (and they will happen if you are in a management position for any amount of time)? My management style tends to favor encouragement and positive re-enforcement but there are times when it is in the best interest of the individual to give them what is usually referred to as a "wake up call". This is always my last resort, but done for the right reasons, although uncomfortable for the employee, can help them move forward. The ironic part (or maybe the most rewarding thing for a manager) is that when done properly the employee, at some time in the future, will look back and be very glad the changes were made. Sometimes continuous learning involves learning a new aspect of the business or altering one's approach to the marketplace. One Manager I worked with who had a twenty year track record of solid and consistent performance was seemingly unaware that his business was gradually deteriorating. Demographic and cultural preferences were changing thereby resulting in a slow but persistent erosion of his customer base. From the outside we all think this would be obvious, but much like the frog, who when put in a pot of hot water would jump out but when allowed to sit in cold water that is gradually heated to a boil will just sit there, this manager (as probably many of us would) kept plugging along ignoring suggestions that changes in approach and addition of different product lines were necessary, changes that came with a pretty steep learning curve. It eventually took a "wake up call" to get buy-in from him and a willingness to learn something new. It took a serious heart-to-heart where I asked him how long he planned to work until retirement and did he have aspirations to take any other position (As a side note; HR would probably have a fit with this as a direct question, but I cared about this individual and his ability to succeed.) to which he replied "about 12 years and I want to continue doing what I'm doing". My response; "what are you going to do if your horse dies before you get there?" He was visibly shaken (the hardest part for me) because he had never considered the fact that his business would not remain viable at least until he had retired, if not much longer. I then proceeded to share with him the facts and figures that substantiated my prognosis, information that when presented logically helped him come to the realization that a change was in his best interest, a change necessary if he hoped to maintain a viable business. This Manager did decide to add the additional product line, actually within just a few days of our conversation. Within one year he was recognizing the benefits of that decision and within three he was generating the kind of growth and profitability that were sustainable. He not only came to love the new part of his business and recognized it as his main revenue generator, but he also proved to be a quick study and an expert in the new segment of his business.

Challenge growth and adapting to change:

I suspect that most of you have already been subjected to various training sessions regarding *change management*, many of which are quite helpful, but at the end of the day it comes down to "things are going to change – embrace it or move on." This may sound cold, but the reality is that once senior management has made a strategic decision to move the company in any particular direction, that is the direction they are going until they achieve success or obvious failure. Now failure is not a particularly good option for anyone throughout the organization, an "I told you so" is of no consolation when you are looking for a job. It is essential that one keeps in mind that, over time, all organizations must change, adapt to their environment, and grow if they are to remain a relevant and viable entity. The key questions in this situation are: First; how am I going to respond to the change? And second; how can I best position this with my staff? The hardest part is deciding personally to enthusiastically embrace the new initiative. This is not to say, however, that one should blindly accept all change because it is vital that you do some soul searching to ascertain if the changes truly mesh with your own values, morals, and management style; not (and let me emphasize not) whether they agree with your opinions and preferences. Hopefully, there have been opportunities earlier in the process to provide input as to the way the change manifests itself throughout the organization or at least your area of expertise (more on this in a later chapter). But once the plan has been formulated, to demonstrate reluctance or even share concerns, regardless of how valid they are, will be considered unwillingness to change or not being a team player. Most people have a fairly easy time making decisions when it involves a values or morals choice since it strikes at the very core of their belief system. Management style, on the other hand, is a trickier subject. I will be the first to say that management style is not a *one size fits all* concept. Although I am a staunch supporter of a participative approach, I doubt a military general in a war zone would have the same fondness or, for that matter, would an airplane pilot in an emergency situation. But the fact remains that most of us have strong opinions on the way we believe people (or we ourselves for that matter) should be managed. You may choose to ignore this, but to work in an environment that clashes with your management style will lead to frustration at work and the real possibility that you will also be rather surly during your personal time. (Good chance your family will think you are a grump!) There are countless stories of individuals who were ineffectual under one system yet blossomed under leadership more closely in line with their own style.

Once you have made the decision to embrace the change, your challenge becomes how to get by-in from the team that you are responsible for? Without buy-in the transition will take much longer, thereby prolonging the discomfort to all, not to mention the fact that certain highly productive individuals may be greatly invested in the way things are currently done and have the potential to completely undermine your efforts. They understand the system and it has helped them to succeed, but it can also give them the clout necessary to strengthen the resistance to change on the part of others. Being a champion for change can be a daunting task; after all most people hate change. However, if you really care about your people you owe it to them to help them succeed and adjust to the new directives in a way that keeps them feeling good about what they do. The key concepts here are: 1. Recognizing that your staff members probably feel very secure with the current methods or procedures, they have enabled them to be successful so far. 2. Many of them do not have the same visibility to overall organizational performance or challenges, nor do they generally have a clear perspective of industry dynamics. 3. They may not be able to visualize how the upcoming changes can improve performance.

Having spent years being the *official* customer complaint department, I have come to realize that the first requirement in finding a solution to any situation is to recognize and understand the individual's problem. Frequently, this act alone will settle an issue because in many cases, people just want to be heard – they want the opportunity to vent. The same holds true for employees who are worrying about change; if we listen to them, demonstrate that we understand their concerns, we then begin to move forward on a foundation of trust. Once people feel they have been heard and understood they are generally more open to ideas and improvements. Of course they probably do not see the change as an improvement just yet; that is where the second point comes in. Our task is to create an awareness of the need and demonstrate how these changes satisfy that need. Sound a lot like selling? Well that is exactly what it is, we need to sell our changes to the group not just dictate to them. I realize this takes extra effort, nonetheless it will pay big benefits later as staff members not only comply with the overall direction of the plan, but actually find ways to make the plan work even better. Remember, as I have stated earlier, people really want to do a good job! Lastly, you must create a clear picture in their minds of how this benefits them, how they can improve and share with them how their improved performance translates into organizational growth thereby helping them to feel a part of the big picture, to develop a sense of ownership.

It is almost a cliché that change is just a way of life and we should not only except it but anticipate it. Creating an atmosphere of recognition and trust throughout your team that many changes are extremely beneficial once fully implemented can be one of the best things you can do for them in terms of protecting their career and helping them to be valuable for the long run. As the Dean of Business at a school I attended once said to me "This will all looks so much better in the rearview mirror".

Make the tough call when all else fails:

Stories of hard-driving fire and hire managers are legend. All too often we are lead to believe that the true mark of a leader is the ability to give orders, demand results, and eliminate those individuals that don't measure up to expectations. Unfortunately, the short-term results generally produced by those managers tend to camouflage the underlying damage to the organization, usually after the wunderkind boss has moved to another position or a completely different company. The reality is that sustainable success is the result of creating a nurturing organization where employees with talent can push the edges of the envelope without continuously looking over their shoulder. The most successful managers (and organizations) realize how important it is to grow their own high-performance employees and how costly it is to replace potentially solid staff members left in the wake of the "success-at-all-cost" manager that just moved on to greener pastures. Now, lest you think we are all ready to join hands and sing "Kumbaya", you should realize that being in charge means sometimes you do have to make the tough calls and I can assure you they can be very tough. In fact if they are not, you may not be suited for the job because unless you truly feel bad about terminating an employee you don't care enough. But, if you do care enough, the best way to insure that you can look yourself in the mirror the next day is to: 1. Make sure you have cleared away all the obstacles to success for that particular individual. 2. Communicate clearly and effectively with the employee in question. 3. Do your absolute best to guide the person in the right direction, whether that is within your own organization or another.

It has always been a frustration to me how so many supervisors are willing to accept the easy (frequently the first) reason for any failure, and usually that reason is poor performance on the part an employee. Statistical analysis and the ability to manage by exception are invaluable tools that no effective manager would want to do without, but *just because it is on a spreadsheet don't make it so*! Learning to take those exceptions and dig deeper to uncover the core problem is an invaluable skill that will help you to stop using Band-Aids to fix problems and find the underlying causes that can be fixed for the long-run. Our tendency, however, is to discount the explanations put forth by the team member assumed to be responsible for the results, considering them to be excuses rather than what they are – insight from a knowledgeable firsthand source. By taking a closer look we can often find fundamental problems that are completely out of the control of the individual we are holding accountable. A simple example is the operating unit that is demonstrating poor performance and whose equipment is frequently breaking down. The manager has been trying to convince his superior for a year and a half yet he does not have the authority to make the capital expenditure for new equipment. The underlying reason for the lack of performance is the outdated equipment, yet it is easy to blame the manager for not handling his department in a way that delivers the targeted results. What the supervisor sees are metrics showing increased overtime expense, maintenance costs higher than budget, and run rates below projections. The reality is that equipment breakdowns are causing work-a-rounds by front-line operators and costly emergency repairs in an effort to meet quotas, all be it unsuccessfully. There is no question that all employees should be held accountable for those things that are within their control, however it is imperative that those obstacles that are beyond their control be identified and addressed by their supervisor. Then, and only then, can you truly evaluate the effectiveness of the particular operating unit and its staff.

It would be impossible to overemphasize the importance of communicating clearly when it comes to performance expectations. Most of us would be surprised on how easy it is to be misunderstood, in fact if you told something to ten people around a conference table, inevitably one of them will understand it differently than it was intended. We are particularly vulnerable when we use slang or trendy colloquialisms that often have contradictory meanings. At times it can also be the result of cultural differences between geographic, socio-economic or ethnic backgrounds. One humorous personal story resulted from a tour I gave of a small manufacturing facility that I was responsible for building and putting into operation. One of our primary vendors was having a group in from South America and asked if I would give them a tour of the facility and of course I was happy to do it. When they arrived, I greeted them and was very careful to remember everyone's name as introduced, to take the time to insure they understood the key points of what I was saying (they spoke very little English and I, unfortunately, do not speak any other language), and to demonstrate how the plant operated and reasons for the particular design. When you are paying close attention to others there is an unspoken connection when there is a mutual understanding of a concept that is being communicated (the opposite of a blank stare) and when this would happen at various times throughout the tour I would give the American "OK" sign (thumb to forefinger and three fingers up). I was a bit perplexed when every time I did this a snicker filtered through the group. As we concluded the tour everyone was cheerful and I thanked each of them by name for coming (I was so proud of myself for remembering all of them) and because it seemed that everyone was getting along so well I felt safe in asking exactly what the snickers were. You can imagine my embarrassment when they informed me that in their country the sign I was making is the equivalent of what we might call "the digital display of distain", "the finger", or "the Bird". Fortunately everyone had a great sense of humor, but it does show how easily it is to miscommunicate our intentions.

When there are performance issues an employee is entitled to a clear explanation of where they are falling short of expectations and what is needed to correct it. All too often they are functioning under what I call a "misguided work ethic". They are working hard to do what they think is best, unfortunately they do not have the correct perception of what is needed or enough information to assess the situation correctly. By sitting down with the employee and clearly explaining the situation we have the opportunity to educate and inform the individual as to the _why_ things need to be done differently. Our tendency is to tell people what needs to be done or how they should do it, but spend far too little time helping them understand why it is better to do it the way we are expecting it to be done. An approach that I have found extremely helpful is one that I picked up years ago reading a book by Mary Kay Ash (1918 – 2001) business entrepreneur and founder of Mary Kay Cosmetics. Although the book was packed with down-to-earth business concepts, the one that I have always remembered was the way she addressed employee performance issues. She used what she termed the sandwich approach – you sandwiched the weakness that needed to be addressed between two positive comments about the employee. For example: "Bill, you are a very hard worker and contribute a lot to the success of this team because of your attention to detail, I thank you for that. Today however we need to discuss something that I think could help you be more efficient and consequently be a benefit to the whole team. Because you are responsible for generating all the approval letters to our clients, nothing else happens until other team members get the logged in letter of approval. Since you are so meticulous in the correctness of the letters and insuring they are all accounted for, you are holding them all until the end of the day when you check each one off. I am sure you don't realize this, but that is holding others up from doing what they need do because they are waiting for the approval. Is there a way that we could do these sequentially so that other team members could get them throughout the day rather than in a batch at the end of each day? It would really help the efficiency of the entire group. I don't expect you to have an answer right now, what I would like is for you to think through your current system and come back to me by the end of the week with options on how we can improve this. Bill you are terrific at insuring the accuracy and recording of these letters, we need to keep that going; you can really help us a lot by developing a more efficient way to handle the process." By starting with a positive comment we let the employee know they are valued. Then we can address the performance concern, being careful to stay on topic and not drifting off-track into gray areas that do not pertain to the topic at hand. It is important to clearly define the issue and why a change is important along with a timeframe for the next step. We then complete the session with another positive comment that enables the employee to retain their dignity and self-worth.

Often times, you as a Manager, actually have a better perspective on what an employee needs to succeed then they do themselves and it is important that you help guide them. If you realize that certain skill sets are lacking, see that they have opportunities for training. When you know that they have aspirations for a position for which they are ill-suited, attempt to give them a clearer understanding of the requirements and day-to-day activities of that job and also alternative career paths. Nothing can demoralize an employee more than unrealized dreams and nothing will destroy a career more than being promoted to a job for which they are unprepared. One of the most significant and meaningful things you can do for the individual and your company is to develop talent and champion their success. One word of caution, however, everyone's idea of success is not the same; never assume that another individual is aspiring to the same things you are. One of the more regrettable things I have done is to recommend that a friend take a particular position that I thought was a huge leap forward in their career only to watch them crash and burn because it didn't suit them at all. Fortunately, they went on to a successful career more in line with their own personal goals, but it made me keenly aware that not everyone is on the same path.

As much as we hate to think about it, there are times when staff reductions are necessary purely because of poor economic conditions. When faced with those realities, there are numerous things that must be considered even beyond the personal hardships of the individuals that will be let go such as employment laws, severance costs, consumer reaction, the effect on customer service and the impact on the remaining employees. Times like these can be extremely disruptive to an organization yet, keep in mind that often without such a move there will be no organization. There will be people displaced purely because they were in the wrong place at the wrong time; they have done nothing particularly wrong. The labor laws of many states make it difficult to only let go poor performers (Of course, if managers are doing their jobs all along poor performance would have been addressed long before a critical situation arises.) thereby forcing a company to eliminate departments or classes of jobs making things equal, but not necessarily fair or equitable. The only possible way for managers to get through this type of upheaval is to be totally convinced that their actions are protecting the jobs of many more people; that reducing by twenty people in a business may protect the jobs of five hundred others. Additionally, by taking the extra steps to handle the terminations compassionately and with dignity we make a huge statement regarding who we are as a company. I am a firm believer that terminations of this type should be handled by the person's immediate supervisor, not someone designated to handle it from Human Recourses. Yes, you may need their expertise present at the time, but the employee relationship was with you and they <u>deserve</u> to meet with you face-to-face. This will probably be the hardest thing you will ever be asked to do, but put your big-boy pants on and do it! If you can't, then maybe management is not your best career choice. I have also found it quite important to communicate the underlying rational to remaining employees, after all many of those terminated were their friends. Trite clichés from change management seminars only serve to anger those remaining, but good honest discussion that helps reasonable people come to the same conclusion enables staff members to work through it. I have reminded myself countless times that doing the right things for the right reasons will generally lead to the right outcomes.

Leaving the specter of infrequent critical responses to changing business climates and returning to our discussion of normal staff development, it is regrettable to say, nonetheless that "you can lead a horse to water, but you can't make him drink"; there will be times when all of your efforts to help an employee progress will be for naught. Sometimes that will be the result of unrealistic expectations on the part of the employee as they want to *move up the ladder* too quickly, so to speak, or it may be the consequence of actual poor performance. Either way, if you have done your job properly, there should be no surprise, but rather there ought to be an awakening of sorts by both parties that this is the correct thing to do. Yes, you will feel as if you have failed, but do not let that keep you from trying just as hard the next time because at the end of the day, the only way you will be able to feel good about yourself is if each and every time you have given your best. And, particularly in the case of poor performance, you owe it to all of your employees to give them a fighting chance to improve. Never forget that all eyes are on you and how you respond to various situations. The rest of the staff are continuously looking for clues as to how you will respond under various circumstances because they want to know what to expect if it they are in a similar state of affairs at some time in the future. Your actions also speak volumes as to the type of person you are, whether or not you are compassionate, understanding, fair - your true values. The health and longevity of the organization is dependent upon good people doing their very best. They come to work intending to do theirs – they trust in you having the intestinal fortitude to do yours.

Cultivating Trust in Management Decisions

There is an old Dilbert cartoon strip (syndicated cartoon strip started in 1989 by Scott Adams) that pictured the pointy haired boss holding a meeting with his staff and commenting "let's hurry up and re-organize so they can't compare this year's results with last year's". As humorous as that sounds, it is only funny because it happens. Frequently senior managers seem to have only one tool in their tool box – organizational restructuring designed to be the permanent fix for all the problems. Unfortunately, these fixes seem to occur too often and with only limited success causing employees to have little regard for the restructure du jour. Isn't it ironic (sarcasm intended) that the most successful organizations are those where the employees seem to have a great deal of trust in their leaders? Not to say that these leaders were always loved, because clearly that was not the case in all situations, but they commanded a certain respect because team members knew they would do what was best for the company and be fair in how they did it. People, for the most part, can respect an individual who is passionate about something even if they do not completely agree with their methods of achieving it, yet they will have little regard for someone who may do all the "right" things only because it furthers their ambitions. We have all heard the expression regarding gift-giving that "it is the thought that counts"; well, in matters of human interaction, it is the motive that counts. Most individuals are keenly aware of the motivation behind the actions of co-workers and supervisors; they can spot insincerity a mile away (Did you think you were the only one that could do that?). When employees begin to sense dichotomy in organizational objectives, their natural tendency is first to protect the organization in spite of current management and second to protect themselves by looking out for #1, neither of which are helpful or healthy for the group. Only by cultivating an atmosphere of trust in management decisions can a business engage its constituents in the attainment of mutually desirable goals. The ability of managers to exhibit sincerity and to willingly solicit the input of others helps to create the kind of trust that is foundational to growth and success.

Senior managers must have the trust of the people:

I am not trying to sprinkle pixie dust here, but I truly believe that to be an effective manager you actually have to like people. Not just those that have certain job skills or credentials, but one needs a true appreciation for people who come to work every day and give their best regardless of job title or compensation level. Think if you will, about where you would place a ticket taker at a movie theater on the job hierarchy; I bet it is not very high. Yet I can tell you that one of the most memorable people I have ever met was doing just that. I can remember standing in line with my family listening to him address each person as they came to the front of the line. He would greet them cheerfully, look at their ticket, notice what movie they were going to see and would then proceed to enthusiastically give them a 30 second rave review telling them how much they would enjoy the film. He did this for everyone, each with no less excitement and this theater had 20 auditoriums! I was totally amazed as this gentleman made the job bigger than we would normally expect. He brought such dignity and personality to each encounter that I was compelled to seek out the location manager to express my delight and appreciation for the quality of the employee he had working for him. Unfortunately, I do not believe the manager was cut from the same cloth, so to speak, and probably did not realize what this ticket taker was doing to give moviegoers such a positive experience at his theater.

In today's "it's all about me" culture, managers who appreciate the abilities and contributions of their team members build the kind of trust necessary for both short and long-term results. Once you step into a management role, your success is completely dependent on the accomplishments of others. Consequently, the more they succeed, the more you do also which seems fairly obvious. Yet, I am always amazed by individuals who are threatened by the achievements of others, who feel that all of the accolades must fall on them. One of the most important lessons any leader can learn is the importance of letting others have the credit. Former President, Harry S. Truman once said "It is amazing what you can accomplish if you don't care who gets the credit". It may be counter intuitive, but allowing others to take credit for achievements of the group has huge benefits in building trust and future performance. Human nature is such that once one experiences the exhilaration of recognition and praise for a job well done; they will try even harder to experience it again. As I have stated earlier, most employees really do want to do a good job and will give you 110% just to be recognized for their contribution. All they ask is that we notice and appreciate them, giving credit where credit is due. Nothing is more demoralizing to an individual than to watch someone else take credit for something they were directly responsible for accomplishing and few things build trust like having confidence that you won't.

One additional element in this foundation of trust is consistency. It is essential that supervisors at any level treat people fairly every day and in every situation thereby creating a secure environment for their staff. For those of us who have had the experience of childrearing, we can remember how experts told us that creating appropriate boundaries and clear expectations helped our children to feel secure and safe; well it doesn't change much as we reach adulthood. Most people feel more secure if they understand what is expected of them and are confident that the rules will be enforced fairly. This is not to advocate a by-the-book, one-size-fits-all approach; people are individuals and must be treated as such. It may be easier to take a cookie cutter approach to fairness, but the fact is, fair does not always mean the same. In a book I read may years ago (I am not trying to plagiarize here, I just can't seem to find the title and author no matter how much I research) the author made a compelling case that being fair does not always mean treating everyone the same, but rather treating everyone special. As individuals, what each of us find meaningful can differ significantly whether that is in how we are rewarded, how we are reprimanded, or what motivates us to higher levels of performance. When employees can rely on our consistent reactions they are free to push the edge of the envelope, explore better ways of doing things without fear of unanticipated reprimands for their efforts and to grow personally in the process.

Process improvement must involve those who are actually doing it:

I seriously doubt that anyone would argue the fact that the pace of change is accelerating and demands that we continually adapt to new technology and ways of doing things. Even those in the workplace only a few short years have more than likely been through a session on change management. Change is inevitable and it is our job as managers to help people through those ups and downs because our staff usually does not have visibility to the overriding drivers of that change. If we are to protect the livelihoods of our team members we must paint compelling pictures of the need for and reasoning behind the modifications and how they can be part of the improved organization. In most cases it is important to remember that it is more beneficial to train and improve current employees than to bring on someone new who will not have the valuable institutional knowledge of the current staff member. With that being said, I am not giving a carte blanche endorsement of all change because, unfortunately, some ideas are ill-conceived. The most frequent reason for these poorly developed plans is the direct result of not involving the people who will actually implement or use the finished project. All too often, projects are plagued by the opinions of those who have what I call *positional expertise* where managers assume they have the best ideas purely because they are in a more senior position. Unfortunately, they frequently have been away from the frontline too long or fail to appreciate the knowledge of those actually doing the job.

The very nature of organizational dynamics is such that the more successful one becomes, the farther away from the actual revenue generating work they find themselves. The bright energetic college grad is hired as a trainee and works at the frontline, so-to-speak, and interacts with customers, hourly employees, and the physical surroundings of the business. As she distinguishes herself is then promoted to an associate manager position, meaning that she is still doing the same work but now has a title. Over time there is a promotion to department manager and then assistant manager, possibly at another location, but for the most part still doing the same work and developing an understanding of the custom base and the employees who know how to take care of them. Eventually, this individual is considered for a manager's position (usually not as quickly as the person would like, but almost always earlier than they are completely ready) and if successful, becomes what I contend is the most important person in the company. This manager is truly the lynchpin of the organization having firsthand knowledge of the customer wants, employee desires, and the competitive environment while at the same time access to corporate concerns and objectives. Their ability to decipher data form either side and keep the information flowing both ways is critical to the success of the business, the satisfaction of the customer, and the overall contentment of the workforce.

So far, so good but from here the career path begins to take on some complicated side-effects as she either remains in the manager's position or continues to advance within the organization. There are many individuals who are not a slave to their own ego and desire for advancement and remain successful frontline managers bringing years of solid performance to the company. Others (myself included) press onward for the brass ring, in most cases with the belief that we can make a difference. What is not generally apparent at the outset is that the two things happen as you progress further in your career: First, the higher you climb within the company, the less direct control you have over day to day activities and second, the longer you have been away from the frontline the more out of touch you are with how things are done in the real world. Granted, early in one's advancement they are able to bring critical insight into staff or senior level management positions; unfortunately we are usually oblivious to when that insight melds into blind spots because we are not in tune to the most recent developments. We become focused on the metrics and less connected to the underlying forces behind the data thereby making decisions that address the nonexistent SKU, we attack symptoms rather than causes.

There is one further frustration with regards to having the proper insight when developing improved processes and that is the executive or senior manager who has never gone through any of what was mentioned earlier. They possess none of the firsthand knowledge necessary to evaluate properly how all the pieces should fit together because they are typically coming from another discipline such as accounting, marketing or possibly an entirely different industry. Now let me make one thing perfectly clear, I am not saying that the only career path should go through frontline operations because there are many highly successful leaders who came from other directions and I will speak to that in a later chapter. But, when it comes to process change, those closer to the activity will bring the greatest discernment and understanding. Effective executives recognize this fact and effectively incorporate their ideas and suggestions.

Process change can be a very disruptive event as it is natural to have some resistance to altering the way we do things. It is the responsibility of management to give compelling rational for the different approach, clearly defining the benefits to be gleaned from the move and to demonstrate a solid understanding of how they change the daily activities of those affected. Only by communicating the comprehensive needs of the organization can there be understanding on the part of the workforce. Through increased understanding, a breeding ground for good ideas is created. Good ideas, when solicited and listened to, enable effective solutions. Effective solutions get quicker buy-in when individuals have contributed to their development and have confidence in those who designed them. Quicker buy-in leads to less angst and disruption and quicker return on the investment. Only when senior leaders recognize their limitations, whether that is from years of absence from the frontline or if it is because of never having been there in the first place, can they understand the necessity of fully involving the people who actually do the revenue generating work not just rely on the feedback of their supervisors.

Stay abreast of changing industry dynamics:

In the last segment I commented on how one might lose some perspective as they advance in their career, becoming out of touch with the most recent developments in the trenches, so to speak. Well in this section I am not going to let even frontline supervisors off the hook. We all have a tendency to fall into comfortable routines that work and have proven successful over time. Whether you are a frontline supervisor, a mid-level manager, or in an executive position we are all prey to complacency, remaining in our comfort zones yet, if we are to be perceived as relevant and our decisions trusted, we must remain abreast of the recent developments around us. Forgive me for repeating the previously mentioned story about the frog who when put in hot water jumps out, yet when put in cool water that is gradually heated will sit there until cooked; our "don't fix it if it aint broke" attitude can leave us in just as much hot water if we are not careful. Certainly one should not change course on every whim, but various macroeconomic influences may have profound impact on your business or organization and can be addressed effectively only if they are recognized early and adjustments are made. These influences can be the changing consumer preferences, advancement in technology, demographic shifts, changing laws or legal interpretations, the local and national political landscape, and global impacts; all of which I will address separately.

With regards to changes in technology, some of which was just mentioned, it is critical to remain well versed in the newer forms of communication as well as the more recent software advancements. This may seem so obvious to the new college grad, but in a few short years you may find yourself slightly behind the curve so imagine the challenge for the 20 or 30 year veteran. There are three main reasons why this topic is so important; capabilities, possibilities, and credibility.

First and foremost are the capabilities of new and innovative software that enhances our ability to sift, sort and compare data in ways too complex for the normal intellect. We currently have more access to information on our smartphones than if we were sitting in the local library; the ability to look up anything anywhere (providing one has signal of course – which is improving daily) in an instant. Certainly obtaining this information is invaluable, but even more so is the capacity to contrast, compare, and comingle data in ways that give us a depth of understanding beyond what was possible before. How valuable are the algorithms that produce the predictive modeling we are so accustomed to and often take for granted; from suggesting our next book purchase to giving us advance warning of an impending tornado or hurricane. Having sound actionable data allows us to make better business decisions that reflect not just the current competitive environment, but potential threats as well. And it is not just the expertise to more efficiently process information that brings value to an organization, but the ability to identify and reach key stakeholders; whether they are potential lenders or investors, vendors, clients or customers. This functionality has dramatically changed the entertainment industry, the publishing world, and completely revamped advertising and marketing as forward thinking individuals and companies utilize these new tools to find and communicate directly with those most important to the success of their organization.

Most businesses live or die by their ability to connect with their customers and our team members who interact with them directly know it. When well-intentioned directives come from farther up the management chain that interfere with that customer relationship, team members are not only frustrated, they also begin to lose trust in future management decisions. The question then becomes; how do we best determine those customer preferences? The answer, as the saying goes "talks easy but works hard". To begin with managers at any level need to actually listen to their staff – the ones that interact directly with the customers. It is the very fact that they are not troubled with complicated financial metrics, economic influences, and organizational politics that enables them to have laser-like insight into customer needs and wants. Secondly, listen to the customer; most of us spend our entire career getting as far away from the customer as possible as we ascend to positions of greater influence (???). Traditional methods of statistically significant surveys and focus groups are certainly important, but current technology centered on easy to navigate websites with customer feedback options (that I hope you actually respond to) deliver faster more direct awareness of customer wants and needs. Additionally, Facebook posts, twitter feeds, and believe it or not, actively and personally responding to complaints will enhance the company's understanding of their patrons.

For those of us who are still mesmerized by the advances we have seen thus far, hold on to your hats because we are only seeing the tip of the iceberg. The capabilities of today are the foundation for the possibilities of tomorrow and I do mean tomorrow. A statement like that used to be rather prophetic, referring to a decade or more in the future. But the pace of change is accelerating so quickly that each new breakthrough is communicated almost instantaneously and thereby causes a figurative light bulb to go off in someone else's mind enabling them to move forward on a concept they had been wrestling with. These possibilities are not limited to further advances in technology, they are fundamental in opening our eyes to different approaches to the way we do things in our own organizations and how we differentiate ourselves from competitors.

More pertinent to the topic of this book however, is the concept of credibility which is foundational to trust. For those of you familiar with Scott Adam's cartoon strip "Dilbert" I probably need not elaborate any further, but in case you are not acquainted with the pointy haired boss I will continue (I can assure you I have worked for a couple of them and constantly check the mirror to insure my gradually similar hairline is not a precursor to changes in my management style). When a manager begins to lag behind the most current ways of doing things they are at risk of being perceived as out of touch, "old school", and lacking the ability to understand the full impact of current situations. The first thing that happens is staff members begin to make allowances for the "boss" and just do the necessary work themselves. This then progresses to various work-a-rounds because now the supervisor has become an impediment to efficiency. At this stage the loss of respect is enormous especially among newer members of the team who have not had the benefit of experiencing some of the very positive things the manager had done earlier in his position. The team begins to marginalize the supervisor as does more senior administrators when they begin to perceive the angst and reduced productivity of the team.

In much the same way as technology, demographic shifts can undermine a manager if not recognized and adapted to. These changes, however, can be much more subtle often unrecognized by even staff members closest to the customer. Frequently the shift occurs over an extended period of time as consumer tastes change, employment opportunities move, neighborhoods age, and socio-economic influences alter the culture of an area. Although staff members may not be any more aware of the changes around them, they will hold managers accountable for not protecting them from the disastrous effects of not responding to the external threats to the business and their livelihood. In many retail businesses this goes unrecognized because staff members still seem to be busy, of-times seeing most of the same customers. What they don't see is the gradually diminishing transaction count or daily sales volume. Frequently normal attrition reduces the employee count so there are no surprise terminations and those remaining are just as busy right up to the point where revenues no longer cover even fixed costs and drastic measures must be taken. Staff members trust management to recognize these trends early enough to make appropriate changes. They will forgive you for making the tough calls; they will never forgive you for doing nothing.

As a leader within your organization, you are not only expected to do something, but you are supposed to have a crystal ball also, or at least to be so well informed that the company can anticipate potential risks. Some of the larger threats can actually find their roots in the political arena. Behind the hoopla of political campaigns hides the ongoing hard work of staffers, lobbyists, and special interest groups crafting legislation that can result in anything from windfall profits to business extinction. The purpose of this discussion is not to evaluate the goodness or badness of any particular legislation or decree, because most of them begin with altruistic intentions, but to underline the importance of awareness and being prepared to adapt in the most favorable way for your particular business. Let me give you some examples:

- The Affordable Care Act – rooted in the fact that we are the wealthiest country in the world yet still have countless people with inadequate access to medical care, the less than perfect legislative results can be attributed to political polarization. Be that as it may, the real test of management is to adapt in ways that comply with the spirit of the law yet protect the livelihood of their employees and the investment of its owners.
- The Environmental Protection Agency – created to address the unrecognized social costs of many businesses particularly in the early stages of an industry. The oil industry is a good example as countless millions in profits were obtained prior to society recognizing that spilling petroleum based products on the ground or in the water caused health problems or that burning hydrocarbons polluted the air. Businesses that adapted early and systematically

remained; those that did not fell by the wayside as compliance costs for companies who drug their feet escalated.

- Social Security – designed to provide a financial safety net for aging and disabled individuals, has now come under scrutiny with regards to costs and the burden placed on future generations. In light of the debacle caused by fixed benefit pensions, what are the best ways for employers to help individuals be better prepared while not adversely affecting their business?

Unfortunately, not all organizations are large enough to have their own Governmental Affairs group or lobbyists, but that does not mean that all companies do not need to remain keenly aware of upcoming changes most of which are not as dramatic as the two listed above. Unless one can clearly see measurable benefits from proposed change, the tendency is to maintain the status quo or when only a negative impact is perceived, to resist it. The most trusted leaders are those that neither demonize nor respond in knee-jerk fashion to potential changes. They are known for their objective evaluation, demonstrated understanding of how changes affect team members, and their measured response to the potential circumstances.

One area that is probably the most difficult to understand and react to is that of global affairs. Discerning how the dominos will fall as a result of significant international developments can be all but impossible, yet important. We have all experienced what the Middle East conflicts can do to our energy costs or how the European economy can affect the monetary exchange rate and the cost of imports or demand for exports. These seem to be complicated issues that should be left to the diplomats and government officials, after all what do these international issues have to do with my little business? Well I have seen small trucking companies close their doors because they were not able to adjust ahead of time to a 30% jump in their fuel costs, farmer's revenues drop drastically because the exchange rate was not favorable to exporting and each and every household find themselves pinched a little harder because the food and energy costs were taking a larger bite out of their budget. Whether world events are causing sub-par results in your 401K or the pizza delivery man is now adding a fuel surcharge; what happens in the rest of the world matters. As managers we certainly can't change these international happenings, but we can make decisions on how to prepare for and respond to them in appropriate ways.

One fact that anyone who aspires to the ranks of management must come to terms with is that you are responsible for others. Your decisions, or lack of them, affect not only the day-to-day contentment of team members but possibly even their very livelihood. Many employees come to work with nothing more than a lunch bag expecting to give you 100% and then go home to their families. Because of your education, training and experience, they trust you to protect them and provide a safe and rewarding workplace. It is a solemn duty on your part to understand and respect this expectation and to earn their trust by maintaining the necessary skills and awareness required of a leader who can successfully negotiate the changing external and organizational environment.

Live up to your commitments:

When one makes such a generic statement as "live up to your commitments" you can almost hear a resounding *duh*.... we know that. But what sounds perfectly simple at first glance is actually much more difficult when adhered to. Of course we usually have little trouble keeping obligations that we perceive as important, however the devil is in the details – what is important? Achieving budgeted performance is important, generating adequate return to investors is important, as is the presentation you have next week to the Board of Directors; but what about the performance appraisal scheduled this afternoon for one of your subordinates? We all value our personal obligations, that twilight tee-time, your child's soccer game or merely the promise to your wife that your would be there at six for diner; but what about that promise to call a customer by the end of the day? Yes, the big commitments are critical, but it is the many smaller promises made every day that build trust within an organization. If you have scheduled an appointment with an employee, keep it and be on time. Think for a moment about the last time you had a long wait at a doctor's office; did you begin to get frustrated and angry? I wager the experience went something like this. You arrive ten minutes ahead in hopes that they may be able to see you early because you have a pressing engagement immediately following your appointment. Once you have registered at the desk with a less than friendly receptionist who never looks up from the computer, you sit and begin to read the various magazines attempting to find those less than two months old. The minutes pass slowly as you finish every bit of reading material available and look at your watch noting that it is already 15 minutes past your scheduled time. For the next quarter hour you fester internally about how your time is every bit as important as this doctor's, vowing to never let this happen again. Sound familiar? Very few things are as irritating, yet are we guilty of doing the same thing to our employees?

At other times it is not so much that we are not punctual for a scheduled meeting, but we fail to follow up on a concern or request of an employee or customer. Their issue may well fall very low on your priority list and there are only so many hours in a day; but where is it on the staff member's priority list? It may be extremely important to them. We live in an age of instant gratification. We tap our feet impatiently waiting for the microwave to finish heating, we acquire information in an instant using search engines, we communicate in moments via cell, text or instant messenger and we send emails and wait at our laptops for a reply. People expect a response even if it is only to acknowledge that you received their request.

Recently I had a personal experience that points out how even the barest minimum of follow-through and communication could have alleviated a lot of frustration. A medication that was prescribed for my son requires that he have a form sent from his doctor annually to the Department of Motor Vehicles so that he may retain his driving privileges. Having been through the dilemma of missing a deadline once before, resulting in his license being suspended, I do not take this process lightly (I am not sure about your experiences with the DMV, but I'd rather have a root canal.). Once suspended a person has to go through a repeat of the entire process, both the written and driving tests.

Knowing that these things can take a while and that the doctor involved is a specialist on staff at a large medical facility, I allowed sufficient time prior to the deadline for processing. Unfortunately, it took five phone calls over a three week period to accomplish what should be a routine request that has been done a number of times before. As a result of the size of this particular organization, each call was directed through the dreaded phone-tree until I finally reached the person who assured me that they were the one to handle my request. They indicated that they would send the request to the doctor and someone would contact me by the end of the day. A week later, after no response, I decided to call back and brave the phone-tree again. I was connected to a different person who gave me the same assurances as the first. Another week passed and still no response. The third call resulted in apologies and more adamant assurances that the third time is the charm and I would be contacted by the end of the day. Needless to say, that did not happen and my next call was to a supervisor who directed me to their patient complaint department. I will give credit where credit is due, this department followed through and the forms were completed and delivered to the DMV, in fact when they checked the forms had already been sent. Let me be clear, this is a wonderful doctor in whom I have a great deal of faith, but the follow-up procedures of certain staff members were unacceptable and actually reflected badly on their co-workers. One phone call, email or text message could have eliminated the entire aggravating experience; instead it appeared that there was no sense of urgency or concern on their part. As managers, we need to recognize the importance of follow through on employee requests. Even when we don't yet have an answer, we can avoid a lot of angst by just acknowledging that we've received the request – then be sure to follow-up!

I was very fortunate early in my career to have a supervisor who understood the significance of following through on small promises. As the first year of my employment was coming to a close, he scheduled an appointment to review my performance for the year. I was impressed by the fact that he scheduled it in advance (even though I was a lowly rookie), was very detailed and thorough in the review, and spent sufficient time to listen to not only my concerns but my aspirations as well. Although performance factors were handled in an objective fashion (there should never be any equivocation with regards to actual results) I left the meeting feeling valued and motivated. Yes, areas that could be improved were addressed, but I was also encouraged to grow as an employee and an individual with unlimited possibilities. Upon completing the meeting I commented on the way the review was handled and he related to me how if he wanted me to take it seriously he needed to demonstrate that it was important to him as well. By scheduling in advance my supervisor had demonstrated that he valued my time as well as his own. By keeping the appointment and being punctual he sent a clear message that this was an important process and by being thorough he let me know that he was paying attention and valued not only my performance but me as a person. This experience became a model for the countless performance appraisals I have done throughout the years, often to the surprise of the employee. The fact is that far too many appraisals are handled in a perfunctory way with little regard for the time pressures of the team member or their dignity as a person. The typical appraisal today sends a clear message that I am more important than you, my time is clearly more valuable and if there is anything you need to know, I'll tell you. Standardized questions lead to routine answers except for those areas of weakness that need to be addressed. The experience becomes less motivational and more a baseline for any future disciplinary action that may be needed, even if that is the remotest of possibilities.

There are other areas as well where small obligations can make a big difference such as timely processing of merit raises or incentives. Another manager I worked for years ago made a statement that I have kept in mind ever since; "you don't mess with someone's money". A fifty cent an hour raise my not seem important to a senior manager who may be making two or three times the annual wage of a front line team member, but it is very important to that employee who is trying very hard to meet the needs of his family. Being late signing off on pay increases or onetime bonuses causing them to be delayed one or two pay periods is extremely aggravating to employees and fosters a perception that management is uncaring and possesses an attitude of entitlement. Most employees will always think a raise should have been bigger (I suspect that most of us are that way) but that is usually not the source of discontentment, it is the act of being processed late that truly angers them. Occasionally, as most of us in management can attest to, there are truly system glitches that may delay a merit increase, but a word of caution; do not blame it on the computer system, the employee will only be more aggravated and assume you are just attempting to shift the blame. One of the best ways to build trust and live up to commitments is to just be punctual. It is rather amazing that the bar has been set so low that just doing what you are supposed to do will set you apart from the norm.

In the eyes of staff members, the true indicator of character in a manager is their willingness to live up to commitments even when they are in conflict with their own priorities. This is not to say that at times there aren't truly pressing concerns that must be dealt with that completely upend your appointment schedule, but they should be rare and of significant importance. It is essential that managers not give the impression that their agenda always comes first or that plans get changed just for convenience sake. Employees will not always agree with the decisions of a manager nor will customers, but if they perceive them to be a person of character they will still maintain an attitude of trust and respect for the person.

Management Perks:

There are probably few among us who do not enjoy the trappings of success, whether that be the house we live in, the car we drive, or the satisfaction of providing adequately for those we care about. Fortunately this does not hinge on us being billionaires; it only requires that we reach some goal we have set for ourselves that is something better than where we were at some previous point in time. For a student, success might mean graduating or getting that first job. Once employed it might manifest itself in that first new car or apartment. As we progress in our careers it may mean being assigned to that choice project or being promoted to a position with a better title and income.

Each of these achievements come with certain benefits that were not available before; once graduated you are afforded the rights and privileges conveyed with that degree, the new job comes with the benefit of a steady income, the choice project may give you a higher profile with senior executives, and that new title may enable more flexibility in your work schedule. Throughout life we attain various measures of success, they can be enjoyed but they should never be paraded before others as something to be gloated upon. However there are some managers who unwittingly do just that when it comes to some of the perks or benefits of their position.

The rub with most staff members is not so much that managers have certain benefits as a result of their position such as more freedom in how they do their job, flexible hours, or an occasional round of golf with a key client; it is the fact that these benefits are often flaunted. When supervisors make a big deal of exiting for that client outing or routinely leaving work early for some contrived reason, staff members become resentful of their actions. Another action that brings out the ire in employees is managers that take the choice holidays when others are required to work. Often times this is the most practical thing to do because many managers are not as up to par on many front-line tasks and would probably be more hindrance than help, but again it is the perception rather than the reality that causes the problem. My father, whom I love dearly and think the world of, was one of those people who thought if you were not side-by-side with him working you must be goofing off. Frankly, that is exactly what many of your employees will think because they do not see the grueling travel requirements or the late night meetings you attended, they only see what you do while they are present – if you are not there you must be goofing off.

The key objective is to manage the perception in such a way as to consciously fend off any misconception of elitism so that team members recognize your commitment to the organization and to them. This is the difference between staff members thinking that you are taking some well-deserved time for R&R or just being a slacker abusing their position. On occasion, let them know about your business activities outside of the office or normal work hours; not as a complaint, but as a sharing of information. When you return to the office after taking that client out, shed more light on how important they are to your business and speak less on how much fun you had while you were gone. Periodically work a holiday or at least make an appearance in order to show staff members that you are not too important to do so or at least that you appreciate the fact that they did. It is not that managers cannot or should not do these things, they most certainly can; it is taking the time to recognize how they are viewed by others and being sensitive to their possible reactions that makes a difference.

Don't assume everyone knows:

If you are a parent of more than one child or were raised with multiple siblings you will understand what I refer to as the "last kid syndrome". It seems that all too often, as we are raising our families, the request comes up from the youngest to visit some attraction or participate in some activity and our response is "we've already done that" only to hear the retort "not with me you haven't". We remember doing it as a family and the family includes everyone – right? - Except at the time, the youngest was either not yet born or too little to remember participating in the activity. This is very much the way it happens in organizations. We think of our staff almost like family and even those newer members quickly become part of the group and we tend to think that they have been around longer than they have. Information, procedures, and expectations that have previously been communicated may well have been prior to their arrival to the team causing them to be completely unaware. As managers we are holding them accountable to things they have never been told or exposed to. Don't just assume that everyone knows; make sure to review certain basics on a routine basis. For instance, send out the company's inclement weather policy annually just prior to typical periods of bad weather or the vacation policy well ahead of scheduling requirements.

      This holds true for long-term employees as well. A person misses a meeting because they are on vacation or out ill, maybe they inexplicably were left off an email distribution list; regardless of the reason, they missed the update or change in procedures. This can result in contentious situations as individuals defend their actions based on what they understand to be correct, only to discover that they were actually uninformed. Customers or clients may have been given inaccurate information based on old directives potentially causing additional expense or complications all of which must be dealt with by management who must either stand firm or make exceptions each of which have their own special set of repercussions.

Employees who feel that they have been unfairly treated because they were uninformed of certain policies, procedures or changes in direction will blame the problem on incompetent or uncaring management. Robert Frost (1885-1977) in his poem "Mending Wall" isn't particularly enamored with fences but his neighbor states that "good fences make good neighbors". Similarly, although we may think some communication is overkill, I strongly suspect that good information helps make for good employees especially with regards to policies and procedures. Insuring that all team members are systematically informed will help to eliminate the confusion, mistakes, and resentment of not knowing. Good information, much like fences, define the boundaries that we are expected to operate within and prevent potential misunderstandings in the future.

Don't assume you know it all:

There is an ailment that afflicts a great number of managers at all levels; I will call it *Positional Expertise*. Generally, managers begin to believe they are particularly expert in various aspects of the business purely on the basis of being promoted to their position although they may have no foundational knowledge in the particular area. This is not to say that every manager in every position must have firsthand understanding of every skill under her supervision (although the more the better), but that it is important to realize what they don't know and utilize the expertise of those that do. For some reason certain leaders consider it a weakness to admit that anyone in their department knows more than they do about anything involving their area of responsibility (and some don't limit it to that area only). They believe that after an hour or so of direct interaction, review of operational metrics for that particular task or department, and a few months of working with them that they have mastered the concepts enough to need no further input with regard to strategic decision making. They fail to see three specific areas where they are vulnerable when ignoring the insight of the individuals actually doing the job; institutional knowledge, team culture, and seasonal or cyclical variations.

Anyone who has ever had to replace a long-tenured productive employee understands the value of institutional knowledge. Those that have been around for a while just know how to get things done. They know how to negotiate the system - who to call, which department does what, how long each takes on projects, who can be counted on to meet deadlines, who you need to speak extra nice to, and the list is endless. This goes far beyond actually being good at their primary task; it is how they make their job more effective. It is not something that can be captured in an employee manual or list of work rules; it is the relationships that have been built up over time and the institutional quid-pro-quo score sheet. In every organization there is the formal line of authority and then there is the behind the scenes network of people who know how to get things done, often in spite of management. These are the people that know their jobs well and take pride in their work, understanding full well that they will be judged on results. You would be amazed by the elaborate work-a-rounds these individuals come up with in an effort to be productive even in the face of ill-conceived systems or procedures. When these employees are ignored or their input marginalized there is not only a loss in productivity, but there is the real chance that they will seek employment elsewhere. Even brining in a new-hire with greater skills will not necessarily improve productivity as they will not yet have an understanding of the inter-organizational network and may well be stonewalled by the existing staff until they have proven themselves to the rest of the team.

Team culture can be a tricky concept because, in light of the most recent spate of books on change management, culture has almost developed a negative connotation. Culture is painted into the same corner as old guard, out of touch, stuck in the past, or resistant to change. I doubt however, that many would argue the innovative culture Steve Jobs created at Apple or the winning culture of the Michigan Wolverines football team who have the most wins recorded of any team in college football according to the NCAA. Sometimes it is the culture of an organization that actually differentiates it from its competitors as in the case of cooperatives and preserving it is of critical importance. Even when the culture of an organization needs tweaking, it can't be ignored. By recognizing and utilizing the expertise long-tenured employees a manger can maintain productivity while at the same time gain the confidence of those staff members as the foundation is set for meaningful and successful adoption of improved methods and procedures. Ignore these cultural norms however, and face resistance and undermining at every turn.

One of the most difficult things for a new manager to grasp is the variation in activity resulting from seasonal changes or volatile business cycles. For instance, people buy more cars in certain months or take vacations at certain peak periods, but the actual month may vary from year to year or the numbers can increase or decrease from one year to the next as factors beyond the control of any individual business can shift demand by a week or two and consequently into a different month. Sometimes this is merely the weather; a week of steady rain may delay some vacations or car purchases for example. Typical budgets rely heavily on prior year performance and project expectations for the next using those numbers adjusted to reflect growth projections. If last year was an atypical year or this year's performance shifted from one month to another due to external factors, the new manager probably has little understanding of the shift and will focus primarily on the variance to budget. This can have a very negative impact on seasoned individuals who are being chastised for not achieving expected performance levels when they know, as a result of their years of experience, that last year sales ran a month earlier than the norm and this year is back to more traditional volume thereby making the numbers lag by a month in comparison. The best alternative is to seek input up front from experienced staff members to create the right expectations going forward, but when that doesn't happen at least attempt to see their side when developing a rational bridge analysis of the variance to plan. Believe it or not, sometimes they're not excuses, but actual rational explanations for the shortfall.

Contrary to popular belief, seeking the advice of knowledgeable people and having respect for those who do their job well, regardless of their title, is not a sign of weakness. Rather, it is the foundation on which trust is built, a trust that cultivates self-worth and ingenuity. Proponents of autocratic styles of management would prefer that you give out a punch list of tasks to be handled then *kick a... and take names*. This neither demonstrates one's leadership ability nor builds lasting improvements within the organization. Good management should want employees that can think on their own without a punch list and to make the same decision in a crisis as you would have made had you been standing there (which of course a manager rarely is). Instead of continually managing to the least common denominator, successful companies will continue to challenge all of their people to be the best they can be and when they are – listen to them.

Create an Organization That Can Be Trusted

Organizations of all sizes and shapes have a personality, an overriding image that resonates in the minds of its employees, stakeholders, and the outside public. Marketing experts will tell you how important it is to manage that image or brand at every touch-point and using every media source available; and they are absolutely correct – but being trusted goes much deeper than that. Some efforts to manage one's brand are so transparent that they actually backfire as people see right through them. When it seems obvious that spin doctors are positioning every misstep in a positive light or (to use a purely political term :) put lipstick on a pig, they begin to erode the confidence of all those who are involved with the company in any fashion. Believe it or not, it comes down to the small things – how individuals of importance in the organization respond in every situation. There is an old saying that states "if you want to know someone's true character, see how they act when they think no one is looking". I believe that is true for organizations as well. How were employees treated during the last layoff? It speaks volumes to those that retained their employment. How did executive-perks fair during the last big cost-cutting initiative? Lavish spending by the boss while staff members are required to tighten their belts sends a very mixed message. What about the pressure put on a supplier just because you could, did that communicate a trustworthy attitude? Each encounter builds or erodes the character of an organization and in the words of one-time Delaware financier John Rollins who died in 2000 "Your reputation is like a fine Swiss watch, once you drop it, it never quite keeps time the same". How a business interacts with the community, if it is straight forward with facts, the respect it shows for all stakeholders, and its willingness to communicate, are all important aspects of building character – an identity of trust.

Be caring and consistent with employees:

Originally I had this section a little farther down in the order of topics for creating a trustworthy organization, but then it occurred to me that the employee relationship is foundational to any image a business might have in the outside world. They are the ones that go home to their families, their churches, their children's ball games or dance recitals and spend countless hours discussing their jobs. They share tales of success and achievement or they relate horror stories of frustration and ineptitude. The picture painted by these employees creates an image in the mind of every listener as to whether this is a good company to work for or buy from. Let me give you an example of how comments by individuals who are not thought to be of primary concern can have a significant impact on a business.

One of my earlier positions was managing an Agricultural Supply Facility that provided many different needs direct to farmers, one of which was Fertilizer. Most of you will not have any background in the Fertilizer industry, but there are dry fertilizer formulations and liquid formulations and I had just completed the construction of a liquid fertilizer plant at our facility. Being the first of its kind in the company, it was a learning experience from the beginning and designed by me sitting in the center of what was to be the plant with a note pad and an equipment supplier parked next to me diagraming line runs, storage areas, mixing equipment and load-outs. As we were nearing completion my attentions turned to actual operational issues and how to best make this plant successful. Yes, we needed to produce a quality product for both farmers and our commercial accounts and yes, we needed to provide timely fulfillment of their orders, but something else occurred to me; we needed to provide a great loading experience for the truckers who came to pick up the product. You see, the truckers that picked up the product were not our customers, they only worked for the people who were, but they had much more influence than one would think more like de facto employees. If they had unusual delays or witnessed even minor mistakes in the mixing or loading process they went back to their destination and complained. They complained mostly because it held them up from making an extra load that day which meant lost revenue for them, but their complaints took the form of reports to their destination of inept operations on the part of the fertilizer plant. The reality is that inept operations translates, in the mind of our actual customer, as poor quality (not to mention he just gets tired of hearing his primary trucker complain). We opened up on the first day of operations with a strict policy that we would make the trucker experience a good one. Get them a cup of coffee, if there was a delay – buy them lunch, do whatever it took to make them want to load there. The result is that they went back home with positive comments and we ended the first year of operation at 2 times budget.

When William Congreve wrote "Hell hath no fury like a woman scorned" (*The Mourning Bride*, 1697) he apparently had not encountered a disgruntled ex-employee. True, some will just fade away meekly, but others – the strongest ones – will haunt you for some time to come. They will be your toughest competition as they work for their new company with a vengeance all in an effort to show you how wrong you were. They know your vulnerabilities and how to leverage them as they subtly bring awareness to your less desirable qualities. You will never completely eliminate disgruntled employees no matter how hard you try, but you can lessen the effect of their disparaging comments while they are with you or after they leave the company by planting firmly in the eyes of all employees an image of fairness and compassion. When these angry employees express their dissatisfaction against a backdrop of a reasonably contented workforce they simply are chalked off to sour grapes.

The point is that people will talk and like it or not, other people will listen. Even marketing experts will tell you that word of mouth is infinitely more valuable than traditional advertising especially in a day where a few key strokes expose hundreds to even one person's opinion. The seemingly ubiquitous usage of social media and the lack of civility or restraint on the part of many of its users can disseminate less than flattering remarks about anyone or any institution in moments. Our employees can be our biggest advocate, positively reinforcing the brand or they can undermine a significant portion of your marketing efforts by creating a dissonance between who you say you are and what the public is hearing at the last soccer game or read on that last tweet.

Be responsive to the community:

There is a saying among politicians that "all politics is local politics"; well I believe that is true for business as well. Regardless of the size of your organization, it comes down to how you are perceived locally. Ford Motor Company is a global business with countless dollars invested in engineering, design, marketing, and distribution yet your opinion of the company often comes down to the opinion you have of the local dealer. The *Holy Grail* so to speak, is to capture the economies of scale of a large entity yet still maintain the feel of a hometown business. This is probably the most difficult challenge for any large business because of the difficulty in replicating a set of corporate values and brand identity throughout a disperse footprint that includes a multitude of preferences, conditions, and cultures. There is a constant battle within large organizations between the proponents of centralized autocratic management styles and a distributive participative approach. In a centralized system replicating corporate values is less of a challenge – give clear direction (usually in the form of a weekly or monthly punch list) and follow up to see if all has been accomplished. Unfortunately, this approach leaves little room for local adaptation and adjustments plus resident managers loose the skill of "thinking on their feet" and don't know how to react when they have to operate off-script. On the other hand, when the system allows a great deal of local autonomy companies run the risk of deviating from the corporate expectations as each manager may interpret directives slightly different. Much like the old elementary school game of sitting in a large circle and whispering a message in the ear of the person next to you and each subsequent child doing the likewise, the message is never exactly the same when told by the last person. This breakdown, however, is more of a symptom than a cause. The real issue for most organization is the inability or unwillingness to maintain quality frontline managers at these locations. Over time expediency wins out when filling positions with less than qualified individuals produces sub-par results in a downward spiral that bolsters the argument of the proponents of autocratic leadership. The reality is that strong local management that is also firmly in tune with the intent of corporate directives can implement them in such a way as to deliver win – win situations, maintaining brand identity and fostering hometown affiliation.

Being part of the community, whether that community is New York City or Mechanicsville, Virginia is more than just a highly visible donation to a local charity, it is the day to day interaction of management and staff with local organizations and initiatives. Not just a transparent - image motivated contribution, but actually being a member of the community; in the P.T.A, kids on Little League, member of a local Church, or volunteering at local charitable organizations. Each and every company associate becomes an ambassador of goodwill for your business because they are the community and help to create a positive attitude in the eyes of the public. This has a number of desirable consequences; it not only helps the public to have a more desirable view of your products, but the company is also perceived as a good place to work thereby attracting the best talent. It has been my experience that those businesses that create a culture of worker satisfaction and local connectivity also have a long track record of success. A self-perpetuating cycle of happy employees creating positive vibes in the community resulting in an excellent local image that improves sales and profits while, at the same time, attracts the best employees who improve company performance and create an even better place to work. I am reminded of one of my favorite lines from an old time Christmas Movie Classic "Miracle on 34th Street" (1947 20th Century Fox) where the Macy's staff is meeting and concerned about Mr. Macy's reaction to their new Santa sending customers to competing stores if they did not have the right product. (Imagine one retailer sending a customer to the competition.) But to their surprise, Mr. Macy had received overwhelming positive response on the part of the customers and decided to make it the policy of every one of his stores - that if Macy's did not have what the customer wanted, they would help them find it at another store. Mr. Macy commented "If we don't have what the customer wants, we will help them find it at a competitor's store. We will be known as the good store, the kind store, the store that puts children and Christmas ahead of profits ...... *and consequently will make more profits than ever before."* Doing the right things are not just heartwarming, they are the best business decisions.

Be careful with "spin":

I suppose it is human nature to want to make the best of any situation; to minimize the bad and to maximize the good. Companies, unfortunately, are no different and utilize Public Relations experts or Marketing Managers to insure that the correct message goes out to the community. This is an invaluable asset to the company because all too often the wrong message finds its way into the public domain and it is infinitely more difficult to correct an erroneous message than it is to inform people correctly in the first place (a topic I will address in a moment). But there are far too many instances where an organization goes beyond communicating accurately and attempts to position their comments in the most favorable light possible. At times these comments can so blatantly manipulate the facts that they actually have the opposite effect than what was intended. How often in recent memory have we heard a politician, when caught in an un-truth (I dare not say lie), respond "I misspoke"? Everyone knows the truth, yet somehow the political leader and their speech makers believe that putting the correct spin on the situation will make it go away in the eyes of the voters. Unfortunately, they are often correct and the same mentality happens in business. In the words of the late humorist W.C. Fields "You can fool some of the people some of the time and that's enough to make a decent living". Of course in his day one waited days or weeks to get published information while today one might get valuable insight in seconds via a twitter feed. I won't go as far as to say that the public is less gullible than past years, although we do have the capability to be better informed, whether or not we take advantage of that capability is another story. The fact remains, however, that verifying the accuracy of information is easier today and more people are doing just that and with a few key strokes disseminate that information to hundreds if not thousands of others through Blogs or Facebook accounts. Our regional newspaper, The Richmond Times Dispatch, publishes each day what they have titled the "Truth-O-Meter" where statements by influential people (typically in the political arena) are checked for facts and rated accordingly on a scale from truthful *to pants-on-fire*. People are interested in the truth, yet often misled by ambiguous statements or outright deception. The consequences of a business caught distorting the facts can be dire as the public loses confidence in their desire to be straight forward and casts a shadow of doubt over everything they do or produce.

Some may consider it naive, but whether an individual or corporation, one should always seek to do the right thing - even if it hurts. Doing the right things for the right reasons eventually produce the right results. When a company makes official statements that are filled with half-truths or neglects to share important facts it not only deceives the public, but it also sends a very clear message to its own employees, many of whom actually know the full story. Even if the general public does not immediately pick up on the inaccuracy of the information, it is only a matter of time until disenchanted staff members share information with people they know outside of work. The damage is not only external; it can be very detrimental to the attitudes and productivity of team members as well. Employees want to be confident that their leaders are people of character and they are working for a company with integrity; deliberately whitewashing the message creates doubt in some and outright indignation in others. The costs are losing some employees who begin to seek other jobs, grumbling of staff members in the community, and a few who will work tirelessly behind the scenes to implement change or rise to a position where they can. It is important to remember, however, that some responsibility for this relationship falls squarely on the shoulder of community. The sentiments of society are so fickle that opinions change quickly and often based on nothing more than insinuation or sensationalist comments. It behooves all of us to validate statements or accusations before passing judgment on any organization, especially one that has been, at least up to this point, a solid member of the community.

Build mutual respect with vendors:

As long as there have been businesses it has been common practice to get the most from their suppliers whether that is a cheaper price, longer terms, faster service, or additional advertising dollars. From the earliest days of bartering and haggling till today where the process has been formalized as procurement (the focus of my graduate degree was actually in acquisitions and purchasing), companies attempt to improve their competitive position by maximizing their relationship with vendors. In recent years, driven in great deal by the Walmart business model, that relationship has almost turned predatory as companies seek to leverage their economies of scale in an effort to garner concessions from their suppliers. While there is nothing wrong with strident negotiations with vendors (in fact it is foundational to running a good business), imposing unconscionable pressure on suppliers simply because you are big enough to do so is both harmful to the long-term viability of the vendor and the image of your own business. This is a deceptively difficult issue as consumers will always reward the company with the greatest value at the lowest price, but the negativity expressed from all those involved can have significant impact over time on employees of both the business and the vendor and in turn the community. When staff members notice what they perceive to be unfair practices such as delaying payments, unrealistic concessions, or lucrative perks they begin to harbor negative feelings toward their employer; there is a sense that something shady is going on. Just how do these activities start?

There are a number of situations that result in undue pressure being put on vendors, not all of them are bad in and of themselves. It is only when they are taken to the extreme that they begin to create the impression of less than ethical activity. For instance; a supplier provides small gifts to their customers for incremental increases in orders. Naturally the size of the gift determines how effective the incentive is, yet it also increases the perception of wrongdoing. A real life conversation I had with a supplier (whose name and business shall remain anonymous) is a great example of this type of activity. I asked Bill (not his real name) "How do you manage to do business with some of the larger companies you supply?" His response was rather interesting. He said "First I insure that I deliver a top quality product, great pains go into insuring that we are the best. Secondly, we pride ourselves on exceptional service. Our deliveries are on time and provide quick turnaround on special orders. And, lastly, I buy the purchasing agent a f…..g Cadillac." Do you think the expectation of a new luxury automobile may have placed undue pressure on that purchasing agent to buy from this vendor? (purely a rhetorical question) This kind of activity sends a message to staff members of both the vendor and the company buying from them that the game is rigged, business is not conducted on a level playing field and that less than scrupulous activities pay off. Activities, as harmless as a nice dinner or tickets to a ball game, can send the same kind of message if they are not coupled with good purchasing decisions that bring value to the company.

One of the more recent hot topics of discussion concerns the health care industry and the efforts of insurance companies to control costs. Granted the need to curtail excessive medical costs in the United States is a serious issue, the details of which are far beyond the scope of this book (or this authors knowledge for that matter), but certain decisions seem out of sync with both good customer care and vendor relations. In particular the efforts to direct all regularly ordered medications through mail-order providers. One can readily see the potential savings of not having to maintain a consumer friendly retail establishment and the efficiency of mailing three months quantity at a time. There are some potential long-term issues however, that may even eclipse the actual perceived savings. The local drugstore has become a valuable link in the healthcare chain as it provides not just the service of filling prescriptions, but a conduit of information and interpretation of medical jargon. True, many people today will do more than adequate research on the internet; yet there are still hordes of people who either do not or have trouble comprehending what they have found, not to mention the issue of individuals who attempt to self-diagnose as they google their ailments. Going even one step further, the local pharmacist provides an invaluable safeguard against potentially harmful drug interactions as specialists for various issues prescribe medications that conflict with something else that the patient is taking that they may not have communicated to their doctor. Many of the pharmacies of today have implemented software that helps to identify these potentially harmful conflicts and are able to alert the customer and the physician thereby avoiding costly mistakes or legal ramifications. Lastly, if you are receiving your prescriptions by mail; who do you turn to when for some unusual reason you are out of those medication on a weekend? One's regular pharmacist will typically assist until arrangements can be made when the work week resumes on Monday. This is not to suggest that improvements should not be attempted or that every local *Mom & Pop* drugstore should be blindly supported; both the consumer and the marketplace are best served by the natural attrition of the less efficient. I do suspect, however, that bolstering the connection between patients and local pharmacies might pay bigger dividends. Why not build on the trust that the customer already has with their chosen drugstore and layer on additional services in a cost effective and controlled situation through partnering efforts between the medical insurer and the pharmacy and use those aggregated partnerships as purchasing leverage with the larger pharmaceutical companies in an effort to constrain escalating drug costs. If insurers continue on the current course they will not only alienate segments of their customer base but potentially eliminate a valuable asset, the local pharmacy, as they lose significant revenue from filling prescriptions.

Another action that, when taken too far, sends the wrong message and is a favorite of turnaround consultants is delaying accounts payable. Let me start out by saying this has roots in sound business practice because many small to medium size companies pay their bills too early, way ahead of the due date, finding it easier to pay them as they are received rather than systematically track the due dates and pay on time. One can see that this practice does not make the best use of capital and exhibits a lack of good cash flow planning as one's company may have had use of that cash for another 5, 10 or even 15 days longer. However, it is prudent to pay bills on time and take advantage of any discounts available, or at least those discounts that are greater than your cost of capital. There are times, however, when a company will be advised to pay their bills consistently 5 days past the due date and still insist on any discounts and refuse to pay any penalties or interest. Granted, this only works when the company's purchases are large enough that the supplier makes the business decision that their volume is worth the exception. Unfortunately, the negative feelings are not confined to the payables department as vendor reps complain to local recipients of their products that they are not getting paid and the vendor relationship is strained. Most individuals believe that their personal bills should be paid on time and expect the same from the companies they work for or do business with. To do otherwise is to give the impression that businesses are above societal norms and casts doubt on the ethical behavior of company leadership.

Anyone who has ever been involved in a competitive activity understands the value of striving to win in an atmosphere of fairness and trust; trust that the opposition will operate within the rules and that you or your team will do the same. These are values and expectations we learn from our earliest childhood experiences and nurture throughout our lives. I have watched Little League Baseball Coaches teach their teams to bend the rules, sending the message that winning at all costs is acceptable. I have seen marketing professionals develop advertising that was deceptive, yet sold product and I have experienced corporations take advantage of a vendor simply because they can. Employees may not possess an advanced business degree, but they know when something just doesn't feel right. Management at all levels must resist the "end justifies the means" mentality and maintain an ethical approach to running the business. More often than not, developing a partnering relationship with key suppliers can be a win-win situation for both parties and as I have stated before, if you do the right things for the right reasons, eventually the right things will happen (I say this so often that it may be the only comment you remember from the book – but that's not necessarily a bad thing.).

Communicate effectively:

Most of us enjoy a good concert. It doesn't matter particularly what type of music you prefer, what is important is that you get enjoyment from listening to the artistic renditions of your favorite virtuoso. As we sit there mesmerized by the uplifting melody or the poignant lyrics, how conscious are we of the work the sound crew is doing? I dare say it never crosses our minds unless we are rudely torn from this moment of ecstasy by the mind-scrambling screech of feedback. Similarly, isn't it disconcerting to finally get to experience a live performance of that favorite recording that you have listened to so frequently that you recognize each crescendo by heart only to be disappointed by the missing harmonies or drowned out vocals? The ability of the sound crew to enable the audience to experience a clear and balanced performance is critical. They can take the efforts of the best performers and make them sound awful if their jobs are done incorrectly. It is much the same way for organizations; they may be doing a great job, but if the message is not getting out in a clear and balanced fashion the company can appear equally as awful.

One can never overstate the importance of good communication especially when it comes to conveying a clear and accurate picture of your business and what it stands for. The ability of organizations to create a vision throughout the company, set goals to accomplish that vision, and define what success looks like is predicated on effective communication. The old saying that "nature abhors a vacuum" also holds true for business because in the absence of information, the void will most certainly be filled with inaccuracy. The best of ideas, when not explained properly, can seem like lunacy and the most well intentioned directives can be mistaken as intrusive when staff members do not get the full story – the "why" behind the "what". All too often senior managers operate on a need to know basis, preferring to withhold information from employees and provide them instead with a to-do list of things that need to happen. Organizations build trust when they share information, explain the rationale behind decisions and help team members understand concepts that may be out of their area of expertise.

Even when individuals are not happy about the impact of a certain directive, if they can understand the business need behind it they will be more supportive of the idea. A few examples may help illuminate my thoughts.

I once worked with a Salesperson who was one of the most enjoyable and exciting individuals I have ever worked with. If we went on a business trip, I always looked forward to coming home because when he told the stories to co-workers about our trip it was always so much more exciting than I remembered. I won't go so far as to say that he embellished the stories, I'll just say that he had a flair for telling them in an exciting fashion. But the fact was that he was an exceptional salesperson who truly had his customer's best interests at heart and bonded with them in an extraordinary way that helped maintain that relationship over many years. Although this person's true gift was in sales, he always wanted to be in operations management and had two quite unsuccessful attempts at doing so. In both cases the result was the same, once he had the checkbook he had no financial restraint. His desire for top line sales led to poor decisions regarding the acquisition of capital improvements to support those sales, resulting in unacceptable bottom line performance. My failure, along with that of others, was that I never communicated effectively the critical importance of the sales function to the extent that he felt a sense of personal accomplishment. And, secondly, that I did a poor job of helping him understand the realities of capital improvements or the effect of turning variable costs into fixed costs. His frustration and lack of success concerning business decisions were the direct result of a lack of understanding regarding the rationale behind them and their long-term financial impact. Couple this with his desire for a career change to management precipitated primarily by a lack of awareness of the importance of the sales function and the situation was ripe for unsuitable career choices. Clearer communication would have either helped him be content and productive in the sales position or at least better prepared for a stint in management. This failure to communicate created an underlying lack of trust that eventually led him to another company where he repeated the same pattern until he settled into a very successful sales position. The real downside is we lost a very competent and productive employee.

Another area that can cause an enormous amount of distrust in an organization when communication is ineffectual is between Business Units or Departments. The success of any organization is determined by the most optimum use of each of its components in an almost synergistic fashion to deliver results. It is not uncommon, however, that any individual unit, in an effort to do their absolute best may be in conflict with other units. This is understandable because if the leader of that unit is good at what they do, they will except nothing less, yet every organization must have priorities. Those priorities may seem illogical to a particular department but make perfect sense to the company as a whole. A very productive business unit may feel as if they are not getting their share of capital for fixed assets while a larger share is going to a developing unit that senior management feels is a potential future contributor or the auditing department is being overzealous as the company strives to manage risk, yet frustrates front-line operations as they wrestle with the realities of the marketplace. Without clear communication from management as to the reasoning for their decisions and priorities, frustration and a lack of trust can develop as talented individuals can't understand why their efforts to succeed for the company are being ignored of frustrated. Relating those decisions to the basics of economics – the allocation of scares resources – helps individual departments understand that it is not an attempt to stymie their efforts but an effort to fine tune the organization for maximum performance and longevity.

Senior managers, if they are to be successful, will do a relatively good job of creating a vision for the future and their leadership team will probably do a nice job of setting objectives, but here is where the water gets murky. The message from the executive conference room seems to get very garbled by the time it gets to the front line. Each manager will have their own take on what they've heard and how to accomplish it and unfortunately many of them will miss the intended mark entirely. This is not intentional, mind you, but pre-conceived ideas or the use of colloquialisms can disseminate unintended ideas and direction as happened with a meeting I had with team members some years ago. I met with my team of 5 direct reports who were in turn responsible for multiple locations and functions throughout the company and proceeded to review the corporate year-to-date financials. I have always made it a point to review the corporate statement with my teams because I feel that it helps them maintain perspective and understand the relevance of their day to day activities to the overall corporate performance. At this particular time the company was not doing very well and it was a time of year when we typically operated in red just prior to our busy season. In my efforts to communicate that position of negative earnings (I mistakenly thought that everyone was as aware as I was) I got too cavalier in my discussion and used jargon instead of clearly understandable financial terms; I made the comment that we were in the bucket for $___. When we were leaving the meeting, I noticed that one of my team members was smiling ear-to-ear and I asked him why? This particular individual was a real "down home" type of person and his response was that he had been thinking that we were not doing very well but was glad to hear such positive news. His take on the comment was that we were doing so well that we were taking the profits to the bank in a bucket. Needless to say I corrected him, apologized for my inaccurate description, and never used slang again when discussing financials.

At the end of the day, it is the transparency and consistency of message coupled with the congruence of related activities that builds trust. When there is a lack of uniformity between what is being said in the corporate publications and what front line employees are experiencing, doubt and suspicion begin to permeate the organization. Employees begin to question if they are being misled or are their leaders incompetent? Who is giving them the straight story, the C.E.O., their immediate supervisor, or their own instincts? They must decide which story is correct and how that affects them or their customers as well as placing value judgments on the wisdom of the directives; none of which improves productivity or contentment within the company.

Too Much Management

One might ask; if I think management is so important, why would I suggest that at times there might be too much of it? My first response would be to quote my late Irish Grandmother who said quite frequently "too much of anything is good for nothing!" I have found, over the years, that she was quite right and that it applies to almost every aspect of life. When it comes to management, overdoing it usually is the result of either one or both of three issues; insecurity at the highest levels of the organization, the overwhelming desire to achieve centralized control or the inability to attract, inspire and retain quality front-line talent.

Insecurity may well be the easiest to address because we are all, at times, subject to its influences. In fact, I have heard it said that if one is to be a good manager it is important to be a little bit paranoid. Although I agree that it is important for a manager to always have their antenna up, being overly distrustful can be debilitating, siphoning precious time away from the key objectives of the group. One of the most unsettling feelings is that of being suspicious of everyone and it can take a toll on the entire team. As an eager and diligent new manager, I uncovered what appeared to be consistent shrink over consecutive inventories. Seeking the opinion of those more experienced, I spoke with Auditing and Loss Prevention gaining little concrete advise other than it appeared that someone might be stealing; but who? Having read a few too many detective novels, I concocted more possible scenarios than a creative writing class. After months of apprehension I was able to identify a quirk in the inventory procedures that resulted in the shrink, it was not theft at all. Instead of obsessing about this non-existent theft, I could have been focused on many more productive projects. Now let's take this one step further, rather than theft, how many times have we obsessed in the same way over someone you suspect of not doing their job up to your expectations? They work at a different pace than you do or they come at things from a different perspective all of which make you suspect the quantity of their work. Far too often these supposed shortcomings are more illusory than fact and should be objectively evaluated, but when we insist on replication of our own set of personal standards we begin to move toward the idea of centralized control.

Centralized control, often referred to as an autocratic style of management, is appropriate in certain situations; neither a general going into battle nor a pilot during an emergency landing has the luxury of consensus building. For most businesses however, success depends upon responsiveness if they are to be customer centric, creativity if they are to be innovators and entrepreneurialism if they are to be market leaders. It has always been my experience that if a manager needed to wait for direction from their boss's boss the battle had already been lost. This is not to say that certain major decisions should not be properly vetted by more senior managers, but most day-to-day decisions do not require such scrutiny it is only the result of insecurity or an overblown sense of self-importance on the part of those higher ranking individuals. I suggest that the better approach is to first, recruit or promote the very best people; second, insure that they are well trained and personally invested in the corporate goals; and thirdly, give them the autonomy necessary to get the job done.

Although it is difficult and time consuming, companies must hire the best talent possible rather than be corralled by paygrades and salary ranges; sometimes the very best fit comes at a premium. Not that this should be taken lightly, there are labor laws to consider, but neither should we shoot scared dice, so to speak, nor be afraid to step outside the box when it is the right thing to do. Once, when managing a retail facility, I was in need of a warehouseman and having little luck finding one at the salary range suggested by the company. A candidate was recommended to me by another well respected employee, but unfortunately their salary requirements were well above the company compensation range for that job classification. As I was somewhat pressed for staffing that position, I decided to hire the individual in spite of the higher wage rate and learned a very good lesson; you get what you pay for. Because this person was so much better at his position there were real tangible benefits that far outweighed the additional salary. Inventory shrink became almost non-existent, rarely was there outdated inventory and customers were always commenting on his wonderful attitude. If selecting the right person can make such a difference in the warehouse, how much of a difference can it make when finding the right individual to put in the manager's chair?

Often times, proponents of centralized control overcome shortcomings in optimum staffing and training by adding layers of management overtop of lackluster performers. Unfortunately, this results in a number of undesirable consequences. The most obvious is the additional expense incurred by adding subsequent layers of oversight. The expense is more insidious than just the cost of salary and benefits, it includes the productivity loss as too many middle-managers, in an effort to stand out to their superiors in hopes of future promotions, send front-line managers in a never-ending search for data and explanations that detract them from core duties that grow the business. A search for answers that, in many cases, should have been obvious to a more senior manager or at least generated by a good computerized management information system. Additionally, these surplus tiers within the organizational chart inhibit effective two-way communication between the highest level of the organization and those closest to the customer or client resulting in poor decision making at either end of the spectrum. And, finally, this extra oversight can not only be directed at the poorer performers (that would make for an organizational chart that was too messy), it results in the same added burden of feeling as if someone is always looking over one's shoulder to the company's best performers. These high performing managers will feel as if they no longer have the trust of corporate leaders and will either move on to other opportunities or remain and settle in to a mediocre level of performance.

    Let me give you one example of how excessive oversight causes problems in the health care industry as the increased pressure to meet financial expectations can result in micro-managing individual areas while losing sight of the bigger picture. A couple of years ago my son was in the hospital for an extended period of time as a result of a traumatic brain injury resulting from a fall from a skateboard. (I have since become the local tyrant regarding the use of helmets) During his three-month stay

I would spend hours before and after work each day in his room while he was in a medically induced coma, speaking to and observing health care professionals. I will preface my comments with my thankfulness for the sincere dedication and compassion exhibited by the actual caregivers; the knowledge and commitment of the doctors, nurses and technicians was far beyond my expectations as each would go out of their way to do what was best for the patient (in this case my son) even to the point of allowing me to listen in to their evaluation of his condition during early-morning rounds. I was truly amazed by the professionalism and cooperative spirit of each caregiver. Any frustrations and problems, however, had to do with the coordination of departments and the administrative functions of the hospital, almost to the point of detracting from the wonderful work of the actual caregivers. On numerous occasions turf wars would be evident as individual departments such as neurology, radiology or general surgery attempted to exert their autonomy and authority in conflict with the physician in charge or patient care for that matter. This would become particularly apparent as a weekend would approach and the physician in charge would request a certain procedure deemed to be relatively urgent only to be told that it would have to wait until the following Monday. Of course on Monday morning everyone is playing catch-up and fail to review the request until after lunch at which time all of the openings for the rest of the day have been filled and the test actually had to take place on Tuesday. This happened several times with various departments and service providers. Having been involved in operations for many years, I recognized not just the resulting inefficiencies for the organization, or the impact on patient care, but also the frustration it created among the talented doctors, nurses and technicians.

As if the undercurrent of inter-departmental bickering was not frustrating enough, the administrative functions throughout the organization bordered on dysfunctional. While doctors and nurses had the latest technology with rolling computer stands and centralized data bases, communications between departments and the scheduling of follow-up appointments seemed to be stuck in the dark ages. Messages did not always get to their intended recipient and a general lack of urgency seemed to permeate the network of office personnel and automated phone trees.

The point of all this is that decisions about coordination, workflow and the allocation of assets were being made by individuals without the foundational understanding of the medical necessity of the patient or the requirements of the front-line caregivers. Operational choices were focusing on cost controls that make sense when reviewing an operating statement in isolation without regard to the comprehensive needs of the patient or the negative impact on their most important asset – their professional caregivers.

Making the effort to staff front-line managerial positions with the right individuals is just the initial step, it is equally important to insure that they are in sync with where the organization is going. Rarely is this accomplished by the ubiquitous corporate mission statement, it is the result of linking the personal goals of managers with that of the organization, winning their hearts and minds. A favorite saying of mine is "I love it when people come up with my ideas"; of course they do not know they are my ideas, they fully believe them to be their own and they are – I have only planted the seeds and they have nurtured them into something better than I could have predicted. Given the right information and the composite value of a particular outcome, rational people will make appropriate decisions. When managers are afforded the opportunity to evaluate relevant facts, weigh alternative solutions and formulate an opinion, they will more often than not come to the very same conclusions as senior executives, only now it is their idea not just an edict from the boss. It is the job of senior managers to share accurate information, plant seeds of ideas and to clear obstacles form the paths of those getting the job done.

Lastly, by avoiding too much oversight the front-line manager is empowered to learn. To grow from mistakes and, more importantly, experience the exhilaration of success; a success resulting not from the execution of a punch-list, but one earned through proper evaluation, attention to detail and wise decision making. These are the very traits that owners and investors want in the leaders of their organizations; why not cultivate them within the company at every level? If not, be prepared to hire outside for every senior position.

Creating urgency without frustration:

There is no question that one of the most important drivers of success is the ability to create a sense of urgency among your team members. Most successful athletic coaches seem to have the innate ability to do this, to instill a feeling of urgency for each game regardless of their record. I had the good fortune to have played for an outstanding high school football coach who was a master at creating this feeling of urgency. Although he managed to amass a winning streak of well over fifty games, somehow he had us believe that in each and every game we were the underdogs. All too often, especially in organizations with a lengthy record of achievement, complacency begins to rear its head as staff members begin to feel a certain entitlement with regards to their triumphs. Unfortunately, many companies will attempt to accomplish lighting the fire of immediacy by layering on additional management to catch people who don't exhibit it. This desire to "catch people" results in two detrimental and frustrating outcomes; first, it encourages team members to spend too much time looking over their shoulders and second, the additional layer of management adds cost and bureaucracy to the business.

A friend and co-worker of mine once said "If we have so many people focused on where we have been, who in the world is looking out for where we are going?" Let's face it; most of us in management feel much more comfortable reviewing performance data and counseling those that miss the mark than we do creating a vision of success and leading the charge. When an organization layers on more management to insure the proper level of intensity each of those managers must justify their existence (and believe me they will). They will look under every rock and find something so they can sound the alarm "look what I've found – it's a good thing you have me here to notice this". When subordinates work in this kind of atmosphere it becomes almost toxic as they spend an inordinate amount of time attempting to not do anything wrong instead of seeking ways to improve how they are done. Most of us feel intimidated when we are constantly looking over our shoulder; we feel anxious and off balance, consequently your very best performers will become unsure of their own abilities and be off their game. To quote Stephen Covey "The main thing is to keep the main thing the main thing" (The Seven Habits of Highly Effective People, Free Press, 1989). Teams are much more productive when instead of inundating them with minute details; managers are creating a picture in the minds of their staff where they are going and communicating the most essential actions necessary to get there. Developing an informed group and building an atmosphere of trust enables employees to move forward in confidence, express their innate creativity and the thrill of the game will actually produce not only a sense of urgency, but a desire to win. This is best accomplished by fewer more competent leaders in a streamlined organizational structure.

Additional layers of management is also an issue operationally because it produces extra cost while, at the same time, brings more complexity to the communication process. One of the challenges of any company is administrative overhead and those that do the best job of containing those costs are frequently the strongest competitors in any given field. However, we will leave the aspect of increased costs for the moment and concentrate on the complexity added as a result of increased levels of management. We have discussed earlier in the book the importance of clear communication, but what we did not bring into the equation is pride and the concept of pecking-order. Think for a moment the times you may have thought about whom should be copied on a particular email. If you neglect to include someone who feels they are entitled to be kept in the loop by virtue of their position, you will most certainly experience their wrath (or at least a curt response). Then of course, there is the issue of placing all the addressees in the proper descending order by title when addressing the email. In one organization I worked for, one's title determined the number of windows your office was allowed to have and resulted in an always busy maintenance staff re-configuring office space to accommodate restructuring and promotions. Please understand that it is important in any organization that the appropriate people are kept informed with regard to important information; the question here is at what point do you begin to experience diminishing returns? As each level is communicated to in turn, there is the opportunity for lost time, misunderstanding, opposing viewpoints, and personal spin; all of which can contribute to frustration and poor decisions at either end of the chain. It is difficult to maintain an atmosphere of urgency when it takes an inordinate amount of time for all communications to make the loop and get response from all of those that are on the need to know list.

A flatter organization with fewer layers of management is certainly more nimble and capable of sustaining an energized response to the marketplace, but it is much more difficult to create and maintain because it requires the best people at every position. Unfortunately, the tendency of most companies is to compensate for weakness by adding supervision rather than correcting the weakness. This always results in a boom and bust cycle as added layers of management continue to increase costs until the expense load is unsustainable and a complete restructuring occurs, frequently with a new senior executive at the helm. I am always reminded of the old fable "The Emperor's

New Clothes" where the Emperor employs a renowned tailor to fashion the most exquisite suit of clothes ever made. The wise tailor knew it was impossible and went through the motions but only pretended to be making the garment while the Emperor and his advisors all continued to admire the work of this artisan. It was not until the Emperor paraded around the city in his imaginary suit of clothes that a young boy was honest enough to tell him that he was not wearing any clothes at all. While most businesses do a thorough job of evaluating the productivity of front line employees, we are less prone to factor in the true cost of a top-heavy organization. The hesitation to evaluate potential excess management is due partly to human nature that seeks and holds on to promotions of any kind and also because most individuals are not willing to "fall on their sword" and express their disagreement with regards to overhead to their senior executives. Often, because they hope to one day hold those positions themselves or, quite frankly, they are unwilling to admit that the emperor is wearing no clothes.

Choose your battles:

If an organization is to remain lean and employ the appropriate number of managerial positions it will most certainly have to leave some things unaddressed. This is almost heresy in our post Sarbanes-Oxley world where we have moved from managing risk to being risk averse. But the truth of the matter is that just as one cannot insure themselves against every possible risk, one is equally incapable of uncovering and correcting every infraction or variation from corporate directives. The key then becomes deciding which things to focus on and consciously deciding which things to ignore at least for the time being. Yes, there are times when you actually have to decide what to ignore. In my first management assignment I was in charge of an operation that was extremely seasonal. During a portion of the year there were never enough people or equipment to accomplish everything necessary yet, the rest of the year much of those needed resources sat idle. Of course this required a delicate balance between costs versus capability and made for some tough choices during peak demand. Frequently this came down to which customer you were going to *tick-off*. It made sense to approach it from this counter-intuitive perspective because it enabled you to control the negative aspect of the bottleneck in capability by insuring it was never your best customers and that you never inconvenienced any customer more than once. Similarly, by deciding which things not to focus on one can better control the risk and hone in on those things that are most important. There is an old axiom that states "If everything is an emergency, than nothing is an emergency" and this holds true when team members are buried in requests from management that are frequently perceived to hold the same weight in terms of importance even when that is not the case.

 One example I found particularly interesting was a roadside lawn and garden business that started very small and, over the years, became almost a landmark. When they first started their building was not very large and certainly did not readily capture one's attention nor did their display of nursery goods. As with many start-ups they did not have the advertising funds to make a big impact either. One thing they did, however was to erect the largest stockpile of bagged peat moss I have ever seen. No exaggeration is intended here, it truly was a giant display, immediately adjacent to the road. Common wisdom would tell you that there needed to be a fence around the pile at very least. And, more often than not, inventory would be better protected from the weather if it was in a warehouse – well, he didn't have a warehouse nor did he wish to spend the considerable sum to erect a fence. What he did have was an enormous attention getter, advertising - whose cost was the minimal amount of loss due to theft or weather damage. Rather than obsess over the lack of control, he made the business decision to accept the potential risk as the cost of effective marketing. In this instance it paid off wonderfully as the business exhibited significant and consistent growth over a number of years as this giant stack of peat moss grabbed the attention of passersby. Nevertheless, to stay true to the business lifecycle, they now have large buildings and warehouses, but sadly no image grabbing giant stack of peat moss.

Choosing one's battles does not mean that certain things are unimportant or that you will never pay attention to them in the future, it just means that our composite efforts are finite and to pretend that they are not is asking for trouble. Technology and the dynamics of the workplace will, over time, alter the things we are capable of doing without additional manpower and even realign our priorities regarding the things we must require and those that would just be nice to have. Bolstering the ranks of management to accommodate all of them at once is no different than if I had, in my first management assignment, hired twice as many people and bought significantly more equipment to insure that the system was not stressed during peak demand. It may have made my life more comfortable, but how long would it have been before the additional expense would have hurt my ability to compete? Just as the iconic Nike advertisement stated "No pain, no gain", the nature of business is such that with no risk, there is generally no reward.

Not everything can be done at the same time:

There are times when tweaking an operation is not enough, dramatic changes must be accomplished. When this is the case, the tendency is to either add additional supervision to insure that changes are made immediately or to bring in a dynamic – make it happen type of manager. The important thing to remember, however, is that not everything can (or should) be done at once. Picking your battles sends a clear message to staff members as to what is truly important. But, sometimes it is purely a matter of timing where even a seemingly necessary task is delayed until a more appropriate opportunity, either because of the natural ebb and flow of the business or the preparedness of the team. Whether you are new to management or just recently promoted to a different operation, it is quite probable that you are picking up on numerous things that you believe should be changed. We've all heard the expression "a new broom sweeps clean" and it is our tendency to notice countless things that could be improved upon. It is also true that the longer we are in the same position we develop a propensity for being less aware of everyday issues, especially if you have made a conscious decision in the past to relegate this particular issue to the "I'll get to it if I ever get time" file. But a word of caution, don't assume your predecessor didn't have some very good reasons for the way it currently is. It can be very embarrassing, especially for a new manager, to embark on some seemingly necessary change only to find out the hard way that the reason it has been done a certain way in the past was because correcting the procedure caused more problems than leaving things the way they were. The most prudent approach is to seek first to understand before implementing a change that most of the team members you have just inherited recognize to be ill-conceived (Been there done that). Frequently, it is merely a matter of attempting something at an inappropriate time such as making trivial changes during an extraordinarily busy period because senior managers are not familiar with the cyclical nature of the particular department or division, alternatively it may be that the proper foundation has not yet been laid for successful implementation. Neither of these situations can be helped with additional supervision alone, it takes an understanding of the particular process, the people involved and the environment in which it is operating.

By way of example, let's take a look at what can be one of the more frustrating of these situations when not handled properly – the *Internal Audit*. There is no question that the auditing process is invaluable to running a profitable business. One should not be so naive as to think that mistakes won't happen or that on occasion a few people will not attempt some very unscrupulous things. I suggest that there are, however, two very important ideas to keep in mind; first, that the focus points and scoring of the audit are congruent with the successful operation of the particular business and second, that audits are performed at the most appropriate time. It is the second point that is most in context to our current topic of discussion. Internal Audits can take up a considerable amount of time on the part of front-line employees as they dig out supporting data for the auditors review and respond to procedural questions. Additionally, those being audited can become quite defensive because they pride themselves in doing quality work and dislike being told otherwise. When this process takes place during a peak business period, it not only is aggravating to all concerned, it is also diverting the attention of front-line staff members away from their normal functions at a time when they are most needed. I suspect everyone is familiar with the term Black Friday, the day after thanksgiving that is typically the busiest shopping day of the year as consumers kick off the holiday shopping season. Regarded as the day that most retailers finally break into positive earnings for the year, it would seem incomprehensible that it would be a day when a company would initiate an internal audit of one of its busiest retail facilities. Yet, various businesses do the equivalent as staff accountants and auditors schedule times at their convenience rather than one more appropriate and less disruptive.

Equally exasperating are attempts to put changes in place before the appropriate preparations have been made or prior to putting together the needed staffing or support systems. When I was a child, I loved to put together model cars and planes. I would gaze at the boxes on the shelves of the hobby shop and select just the right one then rush home to begin. My problem, however, was that once I opened the box I couldn't stop until the project was complete. Never mind that the instructions would direct me to assemble part A and let the glue dry overnight and then attach to part B the next day and so on; I just rushed forward attempting to keep things from separating before the glue was dry. As you can imagine, many of my completed models did not look as good as they should have had I had the patience to assemble them sequentially as instructed. As one might imagine, I have found it equally as difficult to have the patience to wait for the glue to dry regarding the workplace, but have had to continuously remind myself to take things step by step, to make sure one thing was complete before building on that step with the next phase. One of my favorite subjects in high school was Geometry and the teacher was a man who had a strong influence on me in many ways. One of the things that stands out most clearly is to avoid taking shortcuts. I happened to be one of those that could readily see the relationships between shapes which made it fairly simple to go right to the answer of the most basic problems without going through the various steps. Our teacher, however, required that each problem be set up on a page where we drew a large T across the paper forming four quadrants with the diagram of the problem at the top left corner and the problem to be solved written out at the top right. Below that each step of the solution was to be listed on the left side and the corresponding theorem opposite on the right (completely written out, no names or abbreviations). Although this seemed to be overkill at first, I found out rather quickly that each one of those steps became important as we began to work on more complex problems. Invariably, shortcuts led to mistakes that resulted in re-doing the problem altogether. This concept of not taking shortcuts was not only important for Geometry or for helping my children with their homework for that matter, but one of those foundational life-truths that has served me well ever since. Most organizational changes are not simple and therefore require us to forget the shortcuts and build sequentially on each step of the progression.

By first understanding the process and any cyclical variables, one is able to identify key pressure points or bottlenecks that can possibly be improved upon. In addition a more thorough knowledge of your staff not only enables us to identify capabilities but also sheds light on potential gaps. Many improvements will require a stair-step approach as you create awareness of the needed changes, develop the skill-sets required and initiate the procurement process to acquire necessary assets. The internal corporate headlines will, unfortunately, go to the steamroller who takes the business unit by storm and implements dramatic change, but the lasting improvement will come from the individual who thoughtfully and efficiently moves the team forward. We tend to equate activity with progress when that is not always the case, sometime the most effective thing to do is to wait.

Hiring the Right People is Essential

In any organization there will be change as individuals leave for personal reasons, retire or just take another position within the same company. When these employees are good competent managers there can be significant risk in making the wrong decision with regards to their replacement. Angst among the remaining employees can cause substantial reduction in productivity and the adjustment period to the new supervisor can sometimes be lengthy and that is if you have made the right choice. Making the wrong decision can be much more costly and can go unrecognized for an extended period of time. The wrong selection for even a front line manager can easily have a six figure impact on the company before it can be corrected. One might ask; "why does it take so long to fix?" Certainly there can be any number of reasons, but here are a few of the more common situations. First, when any of us make a hiring decision we have a personal investment in our choice. It is a reflection on our ability to evaluate talent, interview properly and to dig beneath the surface of a well-crafted resume. When a new-hire succeeds, we succeed; so it is human tendency to be hesitant to recognize a mistake. Secondly, not all of the issues bubble up to the surface immediately. Administrative issues many not become obvious until the next internal audit, which may be a year away. Dissention among team members often festers for a period of time before boiling over, resulting in the need for intervention from H.R. Discerning a pattern of increased customer or client complaints only happens over time and lastly (but probably most important), you realize that you have lost some good people as a result of their frustration with their new supervisor. There are some key things to keep in mind when trying to fill a position; first impressions can be deceiving, the acquired knowledge of the inner-workings of your organization can be extremely valuable, the ability to adapt to change matters and how well a company makes their hiring decisions speaks volumes to team members about the personality, the quality and the integrity of an organization.

First Impressions Can Mislead You:

We all know how important first impressions are, they set the tone for any further relationship in both our professional and personal lives. Yet these all important first encounters can often be deceiving. Most of us, because we understand how much emphasis is placed on these initial evaluations, do our best to portray the *superlative us*. Admirably, we want to be sure that we have demonstrated our best qualities and potential, but our efforts may lead the interviewer to see more than is really there as their eagerness to fill the vacant position can result in them too quickly projecting the desired qualities on the interviewee. Yes, there are proven interviewing techniques and personality tests that are designed to improve the odds of making correct decisions, but they are not foolproof.

When one is interviewing for an accounting position, for instance, there are tests that can determine skill levels. Likewise, one can be tested for IT expertise or word-processing abilities, but when hiring for a management role there are far too many soft-skills that are not quantifiable. Just how will they react when reprimanding a usually productive employee, what will they say to an irate customer when the call is turned over to them by a frustrated team member or how effectively will they build team spirit and co-operation? It is difficult to discern the needed insight especially since most of us are drawn toward upbeat, energetic individuals. A high degree of energy and enthusiasm can sometimes mask an underlying weakness in organizational and administrative capabilities. Not that those traits are not extremely valuable, but far too often we have hired a great salesperson when what we were looking for was a great manager and the two are not always the same.

Moving a little further along in the hiring process; what happens when we have actually hired who we are sure will be our next superstar? One thing I have found myself guilty of is getting overly enthusiastic about someone too quickly. They start off like a ball of fire, shaking things up, challenging the norms and giving every indication that they are going to make a difference making it is easy to get excited about their suggestions and the things they have initiated. One even begins to question why your existing managers have not done the same things, only to find out that they have been – they have been doing them for years and, as a result of you not being aware, you believed them to be new ideas. I can assure you this sends a very disgruntled message to long-term team members who wonder why you didn't notice these things before and resent the fact that your new shining star is getting all the credit. If one is not careful, being too impressed with the new-hire can undermine their potential success as their peers develop some resentment towards them and it can potentially demoralize existing high performers.

Using all of the selection tools at your disposal is certainly important such as insightful questioning, the participation of knowledgeable individuals in the process and administering appropriate personality testing; but, don't ignore that inner-voice that comes only from experience (experience that comes only from having made mistakes in the past). Once a hiring decision has been made it is absolutely necessary to recognize their accomplishments as they get their feet on the ground and encourage their initiative, but one must temper this praise with a wait-and-see attitude, giving time to truly evaluate the long-term sustainable results. This fosters trust among the more tenured employees and lessens the potential resentment of the associate.

Institutional Knowledge Matters:

It is absolutely amazing how much knowledge an individual employee can acquire over a career. More than just the actual skills required to do the job, they seemed to have a developed sixth sense with regards to getting things done. The longer tenured staff member doesn't have to search the employee directory to find out who needs to be contacted or who is the expert in a certain area; they are probably friends or at least well acquainted already. Because of this familiarity, they can call in a favor from time to time, which will of course be reciprocated at some later date and facilitate the expedient completion of seemingly challenging tasks. This informal network of compatriots transcends departmental or divisional boundaries and just gets things done. I have personally benefited from such relationships over the course of my career and will share one as an example of what I mean. The managers on my team operated under a bonus program that, like most, had some very specific qualifying criteria, all of which were designed to insure that we were incentivizing the things most beneficial to the company. One such qualifier had to do with the proper handling of slow moving or inactive inventory. As we all know, items that sit in inventory for lengthy periods of time can cause a significant drag on capital availability and the real risk of loss due to damage, obsolescence or shrink not to mention how it can distort the underlying value of that inventory on the company balance sheet. If a manager neglected to take the correct measure to handle this inventory they could be penalized dollar for dollar from their year-end incentive on the unaddressed amount. The intent was to maintain focus throughout the year on managing one's inventory and to use the correct accounting procedures to address the remaining items, mainly to systematically discount and sell the items or to write-off all of those left by the end of the fiscal year. In one particular instance, a manger had worked on the necessary write-down items and had sent me the list for approval, but in the haste of handling a few unanticipated last day end of the year items, forgot to actually enter the write-offs into our accounting system. The manager called me the very next morning upset with himself and realized the significant hit he would take to his incentive. Because I knew the intentions of the manager and understood the details of the mini-crisis that had to be dealt with the prior day, I agreed that this was an unusual situation and contacted a long-time friend and associate in our accounting division. By addressing quickly and going to the right person they were able to back the required entry into the just closed fiscal year because the entries for the prior day had not yet posted and the actual books would not close for a few days as final journal entries were made. Fortunately the manager did not have any reduction in his hard earned incentive and the financial entries were done correctly, but the point is that it was the personal relationship and familiarity with the system that enabled it to be corrected, even a little hesitation would have ruled out that possibility.

Knowing the ins-and-outs of one's own company is not the only benefit from institutional knowledge and, arguably, not the most important. In many instances it is the relationships with and understanding of the company's customers and vendors. Entire software programs have been built around capturing this information and making it available to even the newest of employees. The most current of these programs utilize proprietary algorithms to create predictive models that identify customer's needs and buying cycles. Any of us who have used the websites of Barnes & Noble or Amazon can attest to the fact that suggestive selling has become rather sophisticated. But, at the end of the day, people deal with people especially when it comes to the larger key accounts. In my earlier years of direct sales in the field I encountered numerous situations where our offering was superior to the competition and less expensive as well, yet the customer was unwilling to change. I knew our products were better, was confident that our company had a great reputation and, quite frankly, I was a good salesman. So why the hesitation? Invariably it was because their current supplier representative had developed such a strong relationship with the customer. The kind of relationship that makes a customer feel special, anticipates their needs and partners with them when it comes to problem solving – the customer believes that this person brings value to their affiliation.

As companies evaluate staffing needs, it is important to keep in mind the value of accumulated institutional knowledge whether on the hiring or firing side of the equation. All too often it seems the most expedient solution is to terminate or little effort is made to retain a long-tenured employee, but the intangible benefits lost can be significant. I would like to say that the success rate will be high when trying to correct these situations, but unfortunately they will be more like what is considered a good batting average – no one would be disappointed with a player batting 300 - and that may be as good as one might expect on the personnel front. But, the extra effort necessary to fix the situation will pay huge benefits in the long run, not to mention the personal satisfaction of potentially salvaging a career. I have had situations where one department was attempting to terminate an individual yet they took another opportunity within the same company only to be a top performer in their new position. Or, individuals that seem to have all the right background as well as personality yet flounder in an administrative position, only to find out that their true calling is in sales (of course I have had the exact opposite happen also).

I am not hesitant to admit that I am a huge proponent of promoting from within, but I am not so naive as to not recognize the benefits of bringing in new ideas from the outside. Frequently, new-hires can close the existing gaps in certain skill-sets or bring with them key customer insights or innovative industry approaches. My caution here is that we not be so enamored with the new that we forget to appreciate what we already have, it takes balance and objectivity to build a cohesive team. Likewise when bringing on new staff members, recognize the importance of building in enough time for them to properly be assimilated into the organization. Making the right choices in these situations builds trust on the part of employees as well as key customers and vendors. How we treat others is a clear indication to those observing our actions as to how they can expect to be treated.

Adaptability is a Must:

How many of you have needed to learn new skills over the last five years? I venture to say that most of us have had to adapt to new concepts and training over the past six months much less five years. The changing regulatory environment, new business practices, software enhancements and technological breakthroughs are but a few of the things that force us out of our comfort zone. Change is not only inevitable, but its pace has accelerated to an extraordinary degree as we now research more on our smartphones during a coffee break than we used to in the library for the afternoon. Regardless of the specific talents required for the job at hand, can you honestly predict precisely what you will be asking of a new-hire a few short years from now? The more adept we become and identifying this trait of adaptability, the better we will be organizationally as we negotiate the unexpected of tomorrow. Few things are as sad and as wasteful as watching an individual get left behind, unwilling to keep up with or adjust to their changing environment. Unfortunately, because there is a great deal of personal accountability inherent in this issue, some individuals will not be eager to take appropriate steps in advance to help themselves and will necessitate that all companies continue to stress among existing employees the need to remain current. Consequently, it is in the best interest of any organization to attempt to identify those who will; those who choose to accept the challenge and embrace change.

Over a period of time organizations can spend a great deal of time and resources insuring that staff members can perform the requirements of their jobs proficiently. It makes perfect sense to attempt to make that investment in those individuals with the highest probability of success. The issue then becomes; how do we evaluate for the tendency to adapt? Not being a psychologist, I can only speak experientially regarding the various personality tests that are utilized today. We can identify management styles, how one processes information, what motivates them and their likelihood of providing good customer service; I have not seen any that adequately give some indication of one's adaptability to on-going change. From a purely anecdotal perspective, educational levels, especially if there is evidence of continued scholastic endeavors, seems to be the only reasonable indicator and it is by no means fool-proof. I am not, by any means, championing the importance of accumulating and endless array of academic credentials, merely suggesting that a genuine thirst for knowledge seems to be a reasonable indicator of adaptability. In today's environment it is ever so important to have a solid foundation from which to make those changes and the longer one puts it off, the more likely it is to fall behind. I have known and admired a number of people who have started at the bottom and literally worked their way up to a position of importance purely by their own hard work and determination only to find themselves at a disadvantage when confronted by current business trends and fast-paced change. As we move into the future I feel it will be harder and harder for even individuals with that kind of determination to make the same kind of advancement without more formalized preparation.

The ability of employees to adapt is more important than it would appear at first glance because of its many tentacles affecting much of the organization and is especially troubling when it is absent in the management ranks. An unwillingness or inability to adjust to new directives can result in poor performance or undermine an entire corporate initiative. Oftimes it can manifest itself in a passive-aggressive response that senior executives are reluctant to address because of the manager's length of service or past accomplishments. The typical defense, on the part of the reluctant manager, is "senior management doesn't have a clue how things work in the field, so we are going to keep doing it our way". Unfortunately, this cultivates an atmosphere of distrust between an entire team of people and those trying to strategically guide the company. I have even seen it affect how frontline personnel react to and speak with customers. Even if the directives from senior management are ill-advised, deliberately going against them still sends the wrong message to the customers, eventually undermines the authority of the local manager and potentially determines whether or not their particular branch remains in operation. I witnessed one particular company as its local branches felt that they knew better than their parent organization. Granted, their decisions made sense on the local level but were detrimental to the organization as a whole. The local units appeared to be successful in their efforts, right up until the day that the parent company merged with another organization more in line with their targeted areas of growth and closed all the now redundant existing locations in this geographic area. Many jobs were lost and the customer alienation was significant, but the saddest thing was that nobody won because a few short years later the entire company went out of business. An organization benefits enormously from attempting to hire those individuals that not only possess the immediately requires skills, but also the innate ability to adapt to change, to view change through the prism of the total organization, motivate others to see the positives of those changes and work professionally behind the scenes to influence corrections and adjustments that will improve the plan without undermining the entire initiative.

What Message Have you Sent?

It is easy to believe that hiring is simply a matter of finding the right person with the required skills to fill an existing position. In our haste to fill the gap, especially since the one doing the hiring is frequently the one having to pick up the slack while there is a vacancy, it is possible to miss some of the more subtle yet equally important considerations like adaptability, as mentioned earlier, and the message one sends by the type of individuals that are being hired.

As managers seek out replacements, two things (other than time pressure – nobody likes doing two jobs for any length of time) tend to complicate their decision; first, are there changes planned in either the structure or direction of the operation that will influence the requirements of this particular job and second, does the hiring manger actually have a grasp of what the job entails. Let's start by dealing with the second topic. Some managers are not very well versed in the jobs functions of those they supervise. This is not a particularly critical statement because it is not uncommon for supervisors to come up the ranks through some other discipline and eventually are required to manage at a point where multiple disciplines come under one umbrella. The point is simply that they do not have first-hand understanding of the job functions and may well be overly focused on one more noticeable aspect of the work while completely unaware of some subtle, yet highly important facet of the job. Because they have *wowed* the hiring manager, the new employee may join the team with accolades from their superior and leave the impression that they can do no wrong. Unfortunately, existing staff members immediately recognize any weakness and resent the attention the newly hired team member is receiving, in their opinion, undeservedly. Additionally, it sends a seemingly straight forward (yet typically inaccurate) message as to what is valued by upper management. Let us use a hypothetical example: The manager of a particular business unit has worked their way up through the ranks of the salesforce demonstrating exceptional motivational skills and the ability to deliver expected results. The business unit is comprised of sales personnel, logistical experts, procurement staff and an accounting team. A position becomes open in the accounting department as a result of a retirement and the unit manager interviews the seemingly qualified applicants. The choice is a well-spoken, outgoing individual who appears to be a real go-getter. The new-hire begins to make a name for themselves very quickly thereby impressing the manager who proceeds to lavishly praise the new team member publicly only to the disgruntled existing members of the accounting group as they have been correcting the new-hires inaccuracies. The moral of the story; the business unit manager was swayed by the traits most valuable in their area of expertise, yet woefully unaware of the needs of the job function he was hiring, namely accuracy and efficiency. The resulting inefficiency from mistakes and the resentment of the rest of the team weakened the credibility of and trust in their manager not to mention the overall team results.

Another influence on the hiring decision is the strategic plan of management. Any number of changes can be on the horizon such as computer software updates that may eliminate some of the more redundant tasks being performed today or a move toward a newly identified customer segment, all of which may require a shifting of certain responsibilities and potentially adding or removing various tasks. If current employees are not aware of the upcoming changes, they consider the new teammate a poor fit or perceive them to be a prima donna as they are assigned jobs that no one else has had before. Or staff members may become apprehensive as they suspect something is up and ponder how the uncommunicated changes will affect them. Done properly, employees understand the upcoming changes and their implications. Even when they are not happy with what is on the horizon, it gives them the opportunity to prepare, to obtain additional skills that may be more valuable in the new work environment.

Rightly or wrongly, employees observe everything that is done by management and read into those observations all kinds of suspicions and conjecture. The speculation is often disruptive causing unnecessary angst and loss of productivity. Hiring decisions communicate much more to the existing staff members than first meets the eye and their implications should be thought out prior to onboarding the new recruit. As stressed earlier in the book, a little communication from management to their team can go a long way toward eliminating most of these issues.

There is No Free Lunch

Up to this point the comments in this book have been heavily focused on executive and senior managers who need to think differently with regards to their approach to and expectations for managers who report to them, but that is only part of the story. There is a responsibility that must be assumed by front-line managers if they are to expect the kind of autonomy they desire and is necessary of a truly successful organization. All too frequently I have seen instances where managers have abdicated those responsibilities and then were aghast when another layer of management was happy to assume them. Being a manager is not necessarily hard; there are plenty of bad ones to attest to that. But, being a good manager is extraordinarily difficult and requires the desire to hone one's craft, to accept criticism and grow from it then to allow others to take the credit for successes. Exceptional managers take seriously their covenant with not only their employer, but also with their employees and the public they serve. There will be times when doing the right things will come at a personal cost, yet the successes can far outweigh the monetary rewards in satisfaction and self-esteem. The best managers, much like a great coach, learn to take considerable satisfaction from the success of their team rather than bask in the limelight of personal praise. This sentiment is probably best summoned up in the philosophical words spoken by Col. Hannibal Smith of *The A-Team* (TV show 1983 – 1987, Stephen J. Cannell and Frank Lupo. Subsequently made into a movie in 2010 by 20th Century Fox) "I love it when a plan comes together". There is a certain satisfaction in watching the achievements of your group and knowing inside that you identified the opportunity, put the team together, developed the plan and championed the effort, while at the same time allowed every one of the team members to take ownership and credit for the triumph. Now let me prepare you for a cold dose of reality, the degree to which you are able to divert that credit to members of your team will determine the group's success; but the better at it you are, the more even your supervisor will not recognize your own accomplishments. When one is truly good at something they make it look easy – if it looks easy too many actually believe it is (including your boss).

In this section of the book we will take a closer look at some of those challenges that managers face as they grow in experience and work toward being the kind of selfless leader that is a benefit to the company, the employees and, believe it or not, to themselves. To quote former President, Harry S. Truman; "It's amazing how much you can accomplish if you don't care who gets the credit." Individuals who can develop the fortitude to withstand the negative feed-back, discern which battles are worth fighting, not let their pride get in the way, yet still do the right things for the right reasons will enjoy the kind of success that not only produces results, but ultimately leaves them with a sense of satisfaction and self-worth.

There will be push-back:

One of the most difficult concepts that each of us must deal with is the fact that not everyone will agree with us. Sure we argued with our siblings, we squabbled with our playmates over the rules of a game, or we went tit-for-tat with our spouse over where to put the wide-screen TV; but this is work – this is important stuff! "I have spent countless hours on this project, done my research – why do they not see that I am right?" Sound familiar – reminiscent of one's college years and the dreaded Group Project? Most of us, when we have personally invested time and effort into a project, become very protective of our ideas and recommendations. This is especially true in creative disciplines such as Marketing where one can become almost indignant when others suggest corrections to the copy you just crafted or disagree with the concept you thought was a slam dunk to reach the target consumer. It can be equally true in Operations when there is usually more than one way to accomplish the same task or in Finance as decisions are made as to the best use of capital. There is no end to the potential conflicts as well-intentioned individuals of varied levels of experience and passion vie for adoption of their ideas. The key then becomes deciding when to stand firm and when to acquiesce and how to move forward once you make that decision.

Good leaders have a passion for what they do and, as a result, can be forceful when articulating their ideas. It is typically not one superior idea that is the most applicable but rather the creative tension stemming from this dichotomy of ideas that frequently brings forth the best solutions. Unfortunately, there is a disturbing trend in our society today that seems to aggrandize the polarization of positions on any idea or concept to the detriment of civil discourse and debate. Whether it is in the conference room or in congress, posting a check in the win column has become more important than doing the right thing. All too often efforts to reach compromise or to recognize another's position as the best alternative is seen as weakness rather than wisdom. In recent years we have seen countless examples of this behavior played out in news reports across the country as congressional leaders seemingly spend more time attempting to make the opposing party look bad rather than rigorously pursuing meaningful legislation. The same holds true in the world of business where egocentric leaders are more concerned with their image as the one in charge as opposed to seeking comprehensive workable solutions. Ironically, the workplace rewards, at least temporarily, this type of behavior because we are enamored with the strong and forceful leader who exudes confidence only to find out what one humorist referred to as good news and bad news – "the bad news is we are lost; the good news is that we are making great time". Sometimes compromise or acquiescence requires as much courage as standing one's ground; so how then does one exhibit the character of a leader when giving way to the ideas of others?

First let me say that leaders must present their ideas in such a way as to demonstrate appropriate due-diligence and conviction. If one does not clearly and objectively present their viewpoint, their input and subsequent buy-in will be perceived to be of little value. Conveying an attitude of objectivity and collaboration from the outset will set the stage for others to listen respectively to your views on the situation at hand. This is often hard to do because it is natural for a person to be enthused with their own ideas (and can't wait to share them) while internally objecting to the conflicting viewpoints being expressed. The irony is that this very process helps each of us to hone our individual ideas as we attempt to convince others of their validity while at the same time expanding our paradigms regarding potential solutions. The primary objective needs to be finding the right solution. (Notice I didn't say best?) One of my favorite lines is from the 2004 movie "Miracle" (Walt Disney Pictures) about the 1980 USA Olympic Gold Medal Ice hockey Team is where Coach Brooks, when questioned as to why he did not select some of the best hockey players in the country for his team, responded; "I didn't want the best players, I wanted the right ones". Coach Brooks knew, as we have seen played out in other teams, that a team full of exceptionally talented prima donnas is not as successful as a team whose synergies brings out the best in every member. The right solution is the one that has the greatest chance of success given the current circumstances regardless of whose idea it happens to be or if it is a collaboration of ideas. Those circumstances include available resources, timeline, and adaptability. I am a firm believer that a well-executed mediocre plan will outperform a poorly implemented excellent plan every time. Grand ideas look great in a PowerPoint presentation, the true test is the ability to make a positive difference in the organization and move closer to the overall objectives. People will question your motives, others your resolve; at the end of the day it comes down to putting together a track record of sound unbiased decisions.

    I would like to add one little caveat to this notion of cooperativeness and collaboration; you still must find a subtle way to enable others to recognize your contribution. Regardless of how noble it is to work selflessly for the good of the group, in order to increase your access to important projects and key decisions one must be perceived as a contributor of value. By way of illustration, let me share an experience I had as a young salesman. I was selling production products to large farm accounts; products like fertilizer formulations, seed, and pesticides. Most people are not familiar with the complexity of large scale commercial agriculture because less than 2% of the population is directly involved in production (of course 100% of us eat). The process involves testing the soil for nutrient levels, determining the removal values of those nutrients for a particular crop and expected yield, identifying most prevalent pests (weeds, insects, blights, etc.) and prescribing treatments all of which are tailored in concert to a specific program for that farmer and a specific field. The soil test is the basis for so many of those decisions that it is a critical first step and, consequently, one of the first things I would do for existing or perspective customers. Taking soil tests require systematically selecting various representative spots across each individual field, removing a plug of soil from each spot, mixing them together, bagging the final sample, and mailing them to the lab. It would not be uncommon to have 50 samples or more for a particular account and all of the results would be reviewed and recommendations presented to the farmer. On one particular occasion I went through this process as normal, but I failed to do one thing – let the farmer know I was doing it. When it came time to present his program (and hopefully close the sale) the farmer was embarrassed because he had already decided to go with another company. He apologized profusely and said that he was completely unaware that I had been doing so much work. All I would have needed to do was keep him in the loop on my progress. And in case you are thinking that he may have purchased from the competitor anyway; I picked up his account the next season and he has been with the company ever since.

The point I wish to convey is that others are not always aware of what you are doing and sometimes that can have disastrous consequences. The question then becomes how can I accomplish that awareness in a subtle way that doesn't appear to be grandstanding or trying to garner all of the credit? First and foremost, it is imperative that you are good at what you do! Now that may sound a bit elementary, but you would be surprised at the number of people who will show up at a meeting expecting to be heard by sheer virtue of their frequent and forceful comments. Yet, these individuals bring no insight to the conversation because they have failed to do their homework and rarely put their ideas in concise written form such as an email or memo. These individuals can frequently take center stage, but their shining star begins to dim when it becomes painfully evident that there is a lack of substance or comprehension of the underlying details concerning the topic or a lack of follow-through when additional details are needed. The real work begins long before the opportunity to contribute to any discussion; it starts by learning the foundational issues and the real-world applications of your trade. Often, it is the seemingly small or less important things that make all the difference in crafting improvements, even if it is only the ability to identify the pressure points that may be encountered during implementation. However, there are other things that can be done besides developing a solid foundation of learning and experience, all of which come down to effective communication and the respect for the opinions of others. Pre and post meeting emails can be a great tool if used correctly as a way to contribute and seek opinions rather than grandstand. Responding to the group constructively in a timely fashion sends the message that you are engaged and open to criticism. Complimenting others on their ideas can also send a strong message that you are a team player interested in group results. Additionally, just paying attention to the comments of others can be very important. We typically don't think very highly of someone who replies to the statements or emails of others by saying the exact same thing over again, as if they paid no attention to the previous commenter. It is always wise to have a list of the most important points you wish to make, but if the point has already been made check it off your list or at least state that you agree with the previously made comment.

One additional topic that I touched on at the beginning of this chapter was the ability to move on after a decision has been made. Frequently, hammering out the correct course of action for any project can become quite contentious as competing ideas are presented, each individual equally convinced that theirs is the better choice. Egos can be bruised, relationships strained and talented people can exit the process feeling frustrated or even insulted. How then does one move on in a spirit of congeniality? After all, this is only one of what will probably be countless projects that will require the collaboration of the team. A former U.S. Senator was reported to have quipped "My colleagues and I can fight all day over legislation, but at the end of the day we can go out and share a drink as friends." (Possibly a lost art in today's political climate.)The ability to move on, even after a disappointing experience, is critical to not only one's mental wellbeing, but to your ability to make a positive contribution. Something I used to tell myself when I was particularly angered by the outcome of a managerial collaboration (those times when you really feel like throwing in the towel) is that you can't help fix the problem if you aren't even part of the team. Living to fight another battle is an attitude that all successful individuals must cultivate if they are to influence continuous improvement within their organization. It is often helpful to compartmentalize our feelings by learning from our losses but focusing on our wins. Remain centered on the objective and the process, not the personalities involved – don't perceive disagreement as a personal attack on you. Maintaining a cordial relationship with co-workers makes for a more amenable atmosphere at work and, after all, we spend more of our waking hours there than we do at our homes.

Think before you hit send:

Proper communication can do a great deal to showcase your abilities or undermine your professionalism in ways that you may not have thought. How many times have you shot off an email or a text message in haste with little thought to structure or even spelling? Sounds almost silly, after all that's how we respond to friends and family, but in a business setting we leave ourselves open to the assessment of others as well as potentially being misunderstood. Also keep in mind that any electronic communication can take on a life of its own as it is copied or forwarded to others. This may be fun in a social setting but could be embarrassing in a work environment. It is wise to be a little more formal in any business communication and articulate your opinions more thoroughly using complete thoughts, appropriate capitalization and sentence structure especially in an email (people are usually a little more forgiving in a text message). Colloquialisms, slang expressions or abbreviations can come off as immature at the least and poorly educated at the worst. Cultivating the habit of crafting concise, organized and intelligent emails will pay benefits in how effectively your message gets across and leaves an impression with the recipient regarding your professionalism and capabilities.

One of the more common tendencies is to write the way we talk, to be almost conversational in our tone. Although this may work well in literature or journalism, it often leads to the kind of slang and colloquialisms that may be misinterpreted or convey unintended connotative meaning in a business setting. I have received emails from co-workers that, unfortunately, sounded quite uneducated. Luckily, I knew that was not the case, but what about those recipients that did not know the individual who had sent the original – the department head who was copied or the V.P. to whom it was forwarded? Granted, constructing a well written email takes a little more time and thought and I am sure that none of you have an abundance of extra time on your hands; so how can we be efficient and thorough at the same time? One easy step is to make sure that the spell-check function is turned on for your phone, tablet and computer, but please be sure to catch those unintended corrections when the device tries to outsmart you with some totally off-the-wall word substitution. Additionally, when composing important emails I have found using Microsoft Word as an editor to be very helpful (a tidbit I picked up taking an on-line course where format for the threaded discussions did not have spell-check capability). Composing the email in Word and then using the review option with the readability function turned on can give you an immediate sense as to the correctness and level of your writing. A quick copy and paste and you have a well-crafted email that will be more professional. Now you may be thinking, what does this have to do with building trust? I will respond with a question; when was the last time you trusted someone you didn't respect and when have you respected someone who seemingly lacked the skills required for their current position?

Swallow your pride:

We all take a certain pride in what we do; we have worked hard, learned our craft and diligently pushed ahead successfully negotiating life's obstacles to get us where we are. One of the most challenging things for any of us is when those efforts go unrewarded or, even worse, unrecognized. Frequently, as a manager, you will be working with people with very fragile egos, personalities that need to be encouraged, to share the limelight. Sometimes this will seem as if it places you in a position of obscurity as you give credit to team members and, unfortunately, that will be the case at certain times and in various organizations. I can assure you that what appears to be a sacrifice on your part will eventually be noticed by those under your supervision thereby building trust and by superiors who begin to recognize a pattern of maturity in your leadership style, harmony in the activities of your team and consistency in results. Remember, ultimately you are evaluated by the results of your team and, taken even one step further, how your group contributed to the success of the entire organization. Let's take a look at each of those layers individually.

It would seem obvious that group or operating unit performance should be the primary focus for all managers. Most management information systems generate appropriate data to measure and evaluate the periodic results in comparison to budgeted expectations and previous comparable cycles. Today, many of these systems create dashboards of key metrics that enable leaders to make more informed decisions regarding their day-to-day operations. It is very clear that the results of each business unit are important to the organization as a whole yet for operational purposes they are measured individually. If, therefore, we as managers are to be evaluated on the performance of our group we are very likely to be at least somewhat in competition with our peers who are responsible for other groups within the organization or a bit paranoid about stand-out performers within our own team. That being said, most of us are easily caught up in the hype of any new *superstar* that joins the company. This is the individual that comes from outside the unit, possibly outside the company and appears to have had three energy drinks for breakfast and another at lunch just for good measure. They have a hundred new ideas and are quick to share them with others at any level within the organization (especially your boss). This can be a little disconcerting to say the least, yet it is important to be open to fresh ideas as well as to use the eagerness of a newcomer to jump-start the enthusiasm of the existing group. How you handle this situation will not only impact the performance of the unit, but it will speak volumes to your maturity as a leader. When I have found myself in these situations (and it has happened many times over my career) I remember my High School football team. In my teenage years I was a reasonable athlete having made varsity at a younger age than most and always maintained a starting position in the backfield, but during my senior year came a major challenge. Two High Schools were merged and with that came a group of new players, a number of whom were really exceptional. I will never forget the day that Wayne ran onto the field in practice uniform looking like he just stepped out of a pro training camp. The very first thing the coach did was to have him run wind-sprints - this guy was fast! I had heard through the grapevine (we had yet to meet any of the new players) that he played the same position as I did leaving me concerned that I would lose my starting position. That didn't happen, fortunately, but what did happen taught me one of those *life-lessons* that come when you least expect them and typically only reveal themselves in retrospect. Not only did Wayne and I become friends, but the coach changed the offense so that we could both play in the same backfield. The team benefited as we had a championship season and I benefited because that wake-up call forced me to improve my game. The point is that if you do the right things for the right reasons, you will usually end up with the right results. As a manager you must rise above the temptation to want to outshine the new comer and attempt to objectively evaluate their strong points and how they might benefit the organization. Yes, it is important to validate that they are bringing to the table more than just hype, but sometimes they really are that good. If they are one of your peers, see if their new approaches would be of benefit to your own team and consider implementing them. If it happens to be a member of your own unit, find opportunities to channel their gifts in ways that help them succeed and benefit the group. A phrase that I have used over the years is; if you want to be important, have important people working for you. Either way, not to utilize exceptional talent could well be considered the cardinal sin of management (*talk about something that can make you look bad*).

This next area is not as obvious yet actually more important and deals with how the department you are in charge of intertwines with the rest of the company. One of the things that took me a while to come to grips with is that each operating unit has their own report card which may or may not be in concert with overall corporate objectives. Intended to drive optimum performance, these report cards can frequently have somewhat conflicting goals. Rather like the concept of Pareto Optimality where your unit can only improve by having some negative effect on another unit; or, for you economists, the allocation of scarce resources may mean another department gets the funding critical to your goals even when your proposal has a higher internal rate of return. Either way, there are times when you will not be able to have those things that would make perfect sense if your unit was a separate business. Resources such as manpower, fixed assets, and an increased marketing budget may not be allocated in such a way as to maximize the opportunities of your department. Yes, there are times when these are shortsighted and misguided decisions, but more times than not in any well run business it will be because there are more pressing needs in another part of the organization that are critical to the long-term health of the entire business. The great majority of managers will, unfortunately, bemoan the poor decisions of senior executives and communicate to their group how much more they could be doing if only they were given the tools they needed for success. The superior managers, however, recognize that in a company all succeed or none succeed and spend a great deal of time communicating to their staff the *big picture*. All too often we have a tendency as managers to think that we are the only ones that understand this stuff and consequently don't bother to share with direct reports the underlying rationale for less than popular decisions. It has been my experience that this has more to do with the inability of the manager to communicate effectively than the ability of the staff to understand. Helping people understand by way of analogy and example not only creates buy-in on their part, but also builds appreciation and trust. Team members will tend to move forward looking for ways to make the best of what they have to work with utilizing their own ingenuity to improve results.

All of us must learn to deal with our ego and in most cases it is the very source of drive that pushes us forward to new levels of achievement, but it must be channeled in the right direction; learning to take pride in the accomplishment of others, satisfaction in your contribution to their growth and the overall success of team goals. Let me put it in the words of soccer standout Mia Hamm "I am a member of a team, and rely on the team, I defer to I and sacrifice for it, because the team, not the individual, is the ultimate champion"

(http://www.brainyquote.com/quotes/quotes/m/miahamm204528.html#pEl9OjzCYHf3qaRj.99)

As managers we all must learn to take satisfaction in the successful accomplishment of group objectives, content to realize that the many things you did to plan the project, assign the tasks to the appropriate individuals, align the required resources and work diligently behind the scene to provide the necessary cohesion to achieve success. Remember that a coach rarely gets the credit for the win, but he almost certainly will get the blame for a loss.

Getting even is a luxury you can't afford:

Let's face it; we all have a high degree of resentment toward injustice – especially if it has been done to us. When we see it happening to others a certain distain wells up within us, a moral outrage if you will, that frequently calls us into action in some, of-times quixotic effort to right the wrong that has been done. We feel it is our moral duty to at least show support for the recipient of such ill-treatment. While a response to such circumstances on the behalf of others is admirable, it is not so advisable with regard to one's self. When we have experienced an injustice personally our emotions run much deeper, frequently resulting in an immediate outburst that we regret at some later time. Even when we are able to restrain ourselves, all we have accomplished is to trigger enormous anxiety as we mull over in our minds countless times how we might best seek revenge. As human as this instinct is, it pays no benefits, save the momentary pleasure of getting even.

We have an entire genre of books, movies and music that have indoctrinated our culture into the satisfaction of getting even. Heroes and heroines of all ages, after having suffered grave indignities, even the score in some *in-your-face* fashion as we the audience give a collective cry "yes!!!" Is it any wonder that we should feel the best course of action is retribution? To our dismay, however, it rarely if ever is. In fact an overwhelming desire to get even can destroy customer relations, employee trust and the respect of superiors. Additionally, once we move past the initial feeling of euphoria, it typically leaves us with an element of regret for our actions. Let's look individually at all three, customers, employees and superiors.

With regard to customer relations, the idea of getting even just does not work. Yes, there will be times you and your company will be taken advantage of, but how you handle those situations is very important. My first job out of school was selling automobiles and one particular instance sheds some insight on this concept. A gentleman had purchased a new station wagon for his family and two days later returned with his 9 year old daughter to complain that the inside headliner had a tear in it. As he was forcefully pleading his case against the dealership and his assertion that the car was delivered to him that way, his daughter speaks up and says "but Daddy, don't you remember – you did that when you were trying to squeeze our ladder into the car?" Was he trying to take advantage of the dealer? Yes, but one thing to always keep in mind is the lifetime value of a customer. Just as an old coach used to tell us that the only way to get even with the opposing team was to stick it to them on the scoreboard; the only way to get even with a less than forthright customer is to continue to sell to them. There are times when it might be wise to fire someone as a customer, but there is never a time when getting even is the correct course of action. It sends a stronger message to those observing your response than it ever does to the person you are trying to get even with.

Employees, on the other hand, present an even more delicate situation when it comes to pay-backs. Once the cycle of getting even starts it takes on an entire new identity of its own and never seems to end. Think for a moment, if you will, about practical jokes. (I must confess that I actually enjoy a good practical joke, but they do serve as an effective example of how things can escalate out of control.) At one point, early in my career while managing a local facility, we had a blast playing practical jokes on each other. Some of them were extremely funny, like the time I was on vacation and my staff booby-trapped my office. The morning I returned from vacation I was immediately involved with a complaint from one of our larger customers so, as I would normally do, I asked him back to my office to get it resolved. After a lengthy discussion we came to workable solution and to show my appreciation, I turned to open the cabinet door behind my desk so I could give him one of our promotional gifts (I had a built in credenza with multiple doors across the back wall behind my desk) and when I did, every door fell off its hinges to the floor with a crash. I was quite embarrassed, but fortunately this customer had a good sense of humor and yes I did retaliate to various members of staff (They had also bungee-corded my desk drawers and disconnected my phone☺). That, quite frankly is my point, each gag required one in return and can quickly get out of hand. On a much more serious note, there will be times when a fellow employee will do you an injustice and make no mistake, at times it can cause you some harm. Paying them back, however, will ultimately result in even greater harm as you risk looking mean-spirited to those who are unaware of the original injustice or, worse yet, setting off a chain reaction of events that may hurt you even worse at a later time. One never knows where co-workers wind up, which department or what position; their retaliatory comments can cause you irreparable harm. Or, conversely, offhanded comments by you may well cause much more harm to someone else than you had ever intended.

Taking this line of thought one step further, most top-notch senior managers have a good sense for the personalities and the interactions of group members even when they only intermingle with the group occasionally. They are usually very in tune to anything that disrupts the harmony of a group. If there is animosity as a result of unsettled personal grievances, they will pick up on it and you will most likely appear to be petty and vindictive.

Holding a grudge only serves to cause you internal stress and has no affect what so ever on the person who initially caused the injustice. Even if you manage to get an opportunity to get even, it will most likely only serve to make you look worse in the eyes of many others whom you did not even think were paying attention. As hard as it may seem, putting it behind you and moving on is the best course of action. This does not mean, however, that one should not use the situation as a learning experience because it is the bumps, bruises and challenges of life that help us grow. Those things that we would not have chosen to go through if we could have avoided them often prove to be invaluable. Work, as in one's personal life, can of-times present you with blessings in disguise. I can personally attest to the fact that the best things in my life have frequently been a direct result of some of the worst, having been forced in unexpected directions that proved to be exceptionally rewarding. (Please don't compare me to Voltaire's "Candide".)

Do the right things for the right reasons:

Let's expand on the final thought of the previous section and how, in spite of the many unpleasant obstacles that are thrown our way, we are best served doing the right things and doing them for the right reasons. This sounds terribly simplistic I know, but deceptively challenging. If life were only that neat and tidy as to only present us with clear-cut choices each wearing either a white or black hat, we would certainly suffer less angst at the hands of indecision. Unfortunately, we are confronted daily with shades of gray when it comes to accomplishing the many tasks necessary to achieve expected performance. These challenges manifest themselves as customer complaints, employee issues, as well as advertising and pricing concerns; yet how we respond to those challenges, whether in our personal actions or in what we ask of others, will send a very clear message to those around us that either builds or erodes trust.

There was a public service commercial airing a few years ago intended to send an anti-drug message to both teens and their parents. The commercial depicted a teen being reprimanded by his parents as a result of being caught smoking pot. Understandably, the parents lashed out harshly "where did you learn to do such a thing!" and the young man responded "from you" catching both the parents and the viewers by surprise. The point being that others are watching us when we are unaware that they are doing so and the influence of our actions can certainly have unintended consequences. In the workplace, employees are taking cues from their supervisors, watching the things they do or say and modify their own actions accordingly. I have frequently coached managers to pay attention to the affect that even just their mood has on the temperament of the entire staff; because if the manager comes in with a surly disposition, staff members are more than likely going to follow suit. The very same principle holds true for doing the right things for the right reasons. If staff members see managers making decisions for purely monetary reasons or expediency sake rather than for what is appropriate, they will begin to question the underlying motives and integrity of their leaders or, worse yet, they may begin to mimic what they see.

Now what exactly do I mean by doing the right things for the right reasons? Let's start with doing the right things. One area of business that is ripe with opportunities to go astray of doing the right things is handling customer complaints. Customers complain for any number of reasons, some valid – some not, but how we handle them is very telling with regards to the character of an organization. Many organizations begin any complaint call with the attitude that "we cannot possibly have done anything wrong" thereby entering into the conversation in a defensive posture. (For any of us who are married or in a serious relationship, we know how that torpedoes any hope of productive discourse.) Companies, through the actions and attitudes of their managers, can create a culture that stymies any conversation much less investigation as to what the real issues are surrounding the complaint. When our leaders are so myopic in their views that they refuse to even entertain the idea that there could be some validity in a complaint, they send a strong message to staff members on how they should be handling subsequent customer inquiries. Doing the right thing would be to politely engage the customer in discussion assuring them that your company is committed to taking the appropriate corrective action, but in order to do that you just need to get all the information necessary to assist them in correcting the issue.

Developing this type of response by frontline staff members only occurs when they have witnessed it in the behaviors of their supervisors; when they see their managers do the right thing even if it hurts. Just because the solution is costly does not eliminate it from being the correct thing to do and demonstrating the willingness to do what is right sends a powerful message to employees and customers alike.

Let me give you an example of what I mean. I am sure that very few of you are familiar with the workings of a feed mill, however most of us have pets and we routinely purchase bags of food for those lovable adopted family members. Well the same manufacturing facility that makes the pet food you purchase may also make livestock feed for farm animals of all types. Typically, the manufacturing of pet food was an off-shoot of the formulating of livestock feed in the first place. Never the less, the same exacting procedures and safeguards that we expect in our pet food goes into the making of livestock feed and there are strict quality controls in place. The feed quality has a direct bearing on the health and productivity of the particular farm animals and the profitability of the farmer. This is such a big deal, that mill managers are graded on their adherence to formulation standards and the integrity of their storage facilities. This particular incidence involved a farmer who upon receiving a shipment of bulk feed (large quantity users will get feed delivered in bulk and stored in bins for automated distribution when needed rather than small individual bags.) noticed that there were feathers in his feed. This can be a rather significant problem as contaminants of any kind can have a negative impact on anything that is related to the food chain. When this was brought to the attention of the mill, the initial response was that it had to have happened at the farmer's site because the mill had such stringent controls in place that it couldn't have happened there. When a second complaint came in, the mill manager sent someone out to the farm to inspect their storage facility only to find nothing wrong. Meanwhile the customer had been informed by his regular delivery driver that the mill actually did seem to have a real issues with pigeons and subsequently relayed this information back to the manager at the mill. Reluctantly, the manager inspected his own facility only to find out, much to his surprise, that he did, in fact, have a problem with a small hole in a storage tank that allowed birds to get in but rarely could they get out. The unfortunate part about all of this was twofold; first it diminished the confidence the customer had with the manufacturer and secondly, it became more costly to settle the complaint than it would have if the mill had been open-minded in the first place and just apologized. More importantly, the attitude of the mill manager sent a clear message to those around him as to how such matters should be handled; a problem that, when not addressed, may persist for quite a long period of time.

At times, however, contrary to common belief; the customer is not right and our front-line employees know it. All too often the staff member has communicated the inaccuracy or absurdity of the customer demands to higher-ups only to fall on deaf ears and a more senior manager submits to the unwarranted demands of the customer. I can assure you that this absolutely infuriates some of your best people who take it as criticism of their own judgment and ability. If you want to truly develop trust within your organization, be willing to back your employee when it is appropriate to do so. Senior managers have a tendency to just want to make the problem go away – your employees are viewing it through the eyes of a dedicated staff member who's judgment and experience is now being questioned. If there are times when the best business decision is to agree to the unwarranted demands (which is frequently the case), be sure to have a conversation with the concerned employee letting them know how much they are valued and the decision had nothing to do with the validity of the complaint and certainly nothing to do with their assessment of the situation. When management sets the right tone with regards to handling complaints, employees are not only empowered to handle them quickly but they are more willing to go the extra mile because they feel that their supervisors have confidence in them and the decisions they make.

Employee issues can also generate a multitude of opportunities when it comes to doing the right things for the right reasons. In most "Right to Work" states employers are not required to give a specific reason for termination as long as the termination does not violate any E.E.O.C. laws so, consequently, the easiest course of action may be to fire an individual who is perceived to be the root of some problem. Yes, there are times when this is the best thing to do and certainly the most expedient, but is it the most beneficial choice for the organization in the long run? Although it takes more time and effort to dig into the details by interviewing affected individuals or witnesses, the benefits far outweigh the additional time spent. By investigating thoroughly, you send a clear message of fairness to the employee in question as well as to their co-workers not to mention reducing the chance of terminating an otherwise good worker by mistake. Of course many companies, if for no other reason, realize that mishandling of these issues can be expensive. Wrongful discharge suits can be costly with even minor ones costing in excess of $10,000 - $20,000 just to prove you were right in the first place not to mention how bad it can get if it is a particularly questionable decision.

The downside of mishandling employee issues is so costly in terms of legal expenses and employee morale that it is somewhat of a no-brainer to be compassionate (Lest the reader think that I am a total bleeding heart, it actually makes good financial sense to be caring and considerate.) It is better to make a few mistakes by trying; after all, the worst problem is that you have an unsatisfactory employee for a little while longer. The upside is that your team will see a certain level of fairness and believe they work for a company that cares enough to do what is necessary to uncover the facts and make the appropriate decisions. Frequently, this instills a sense of pride and ownership on the part of the team who, in turn, police themselves for ne'er-do-wells and weed them out for you. It has been my experience that even when you have an employee who is a legitimate problem, doing the right things for the right reasons eventually boxes them into a corner and they will leave on their own accord with much less fuss.

Another area ripe with challenges is advertising and along with it the building of one's brand. Because of the shenanigans of early era marketing efforts the mere term connotes deceptiveness and chicanery. The truth, however, is that advertising is absolutely essential for any entity to attract clients or customers; customers that now are much more sophisticated than many years past. Because it is so essential, evidenced by somewhere in the neighborhood of $500 billion spent annually worldwide (Statista website - http://www.statista.com/statistics/273288/advertising-spending-worldwide/) there is an almost overwhelming temptation to overstate or aggrandize one's message. Unfortunately, this behavior is too frequently rewarded as uninformed individuals make choices predicated on faulty information and deceptive promises. The most calloused among us would decry "caveat emptor", but we must admit that there is a widening divide between educational levels and access to information. Those with additional learning experiences and are adept with current technology have the ability to research these claims and make informed decisions. In these instances a company making false or exaggerated claims becomes suspect in the mind of the consumer resulting in a negative response as opposed to the intent of the advertiser. Regrettably, there are those without the same advantages whether by circumstance, age or by choice who fall prey to the bogus claims of unscrupulous entities. Yes, to some extent this has held true since the first bartered exchange in ancient times, but that does not relieve us from the obligation to protect those who are most susceptible to abuse. Nor does it eliminate the harm done to any trusting relationship, be that a customer, vendor or employee.

The nice thing about doing the right things for the right reasons, with regard to advertising, is that it is actually profitable to do so. People actually do respond to truthfulness and integrity, sure there is always be an element that will make their decisions solely on price, but the majority eventually realize that a cheap price is rarely the best value. This became quite clear to me at one point in my career as a particular competitor was using some rather deceptive approaches in their promotional material. Not than any of the things they mentioned were actually untrue, they just failed to convey the complete picture. Teaser pricing, well below their competition, was used to attract new customers who then signed on to an extended period of service. What was not apparent to the newly acquired consumer was the plethora of additional fees and charges that negated any of the perceived up-front savings and that their arrangement with the company was extremely hard to terminate. In a relatively short period of time these buyers became frustrated and angry as they realized that they had been misled and were actually paying more than they would have through comparable alternatives. The company I worked for recognized that there was a significant amount of consumer backlash to this competitor's practices that were almost the polar opposite of our own. This company, while always posting a cheap price, had built in so many exclusions and exceptions that customers were beginning to feel as if they had been taken advantage of or at least deceived. Although we had initially been outmaneuvered by some of these offers, once we were able to tactfully contrast our practices with that of this other company in the minds of potential customers, it became a windfall of new accounts. Ours had always been a straight forward – what you see is what you get approach to the marketplace feeling that an informed customer is a long-term customer; the challenge is how do you effectively convey that to the marketplace? Consequently, we developed an advertising strategy around "no games, no gimmicks" thereby calling attention not only to our straightforward way of doing business, but also to the deceptive practices of some of our competitors. We were validating our own integrity not just to our current and potential customers, but to our own employees as well.

The final area I will discuss in the context of doing the right things for the right reasons is pricing. I doubt I would get much disagreement that pricing is more competitive today than in the past. Whether it is a search engine that seeks out the best price, a website that creates bid/offer atmosphere or and app on our phone that scans barcodes and generates pricing for that item in the surrounding area; price discovery is a much easier and thorough process. Unfortunately, the price is not always the price as retailers place exclusions in the fine print (as mentioned earlier) or as they use algorithms to identify the most likely add-on items that will be sold at higher margins. Basically, this is a sophisticated version of "would you like fries with that" and places the most tempting items in front of the customer for their consideration. I am sure we could gather enough material for another book just on the discussion surrounding the competing viewpoints as to whether this is an invaluable tool for the customer or an exceedingly intrusive contrivance for the seller. Suffice it to say that there are a multitude of examples where this technology can be misapplied to deceive the customer. Firms that have done so have, for all practical purposes, forced most companies to follow their lead if for any other reason self-defense.

Let me give an example of what I mean: Company "A" has advertised a very popular widget for $49.95 and company "B" is priced at $53.95. It would appear that company "A" is the clear choice except when the buyer attempts to make the purchase they are informed of the restrictions and exclusions. Whereas company "B" has very transparent pricing and no conditions, company "A" will only sell one to a customer (this customer needed two and the price for the second item reverted to the original $58.95 making two items from retailer "B" actually a little cheaper) and the price only applies if it is put on their own proprietary credit card (one that charges in excess of 18% interest). Retailers with straight forward pricing are put at a disadvantage unless; 1. They give in and do the same thing, 2. They can get their straight forward message out or 3. Are content to catch customers on the rebound at which time they usually wind up with a very loyal and trusting customer. The unfortunate fact, however, is that many business today are either highly leveraged or driven by stock valuations to the point that they can't afford the patience to wait for option #3. Equally challenging is option#2 because advertising can be very expensive, especially when attempting to sway public opinion rather than just catch their attention with a price. Unfortunately, this leaves option #1 as an attractive choice even if it does pose some very negative repercussions.

It has been my experience that making the effort to do things for the right reasons does, over time, produce the best results. The challenge, of course, is to survive until you get there. In a time where investors seek instant returns, it is difficult to maintain the strategic posture of long-term growth and market stability even if it is the most financially rewarding in the long run.

Let me pose an analogy, if I may, using commodity hedging by a procurement department for their resale outlets as an example of what I mean. It has always been my contention that over the long-term (let us say 10 years) an un-hedged position can potentially return the greatest total profitability in terms of aggregate wholesale and retail margins. The problem, however, is that most companies cannot withstand the interim market swings and potential losses that may be compressed into a very short time period, so they must resort to hedging as a means to manage that risk. Basically, this is an insurance policy and, as with all insurance policies, there is a cost involved; either the direct trading costs or the opportunity costs of being on the wrong side of the hedge. Returning to our topic of pricing (it can also apply to advertising, for that matter), most businesses feel the competitive pressure of some of the games and gimmicks and must resort to mimicking their behavior as a sort of insurance policy against loses in market share even when long-term results would be better if they did not.

I have always found that one of the greatest determinants of success is the ability to force oneself to do those things that we don't find easy to do. We learn very early in elementary school that homework may not be fun, but those that do it succeed. As we become involved in extracurricular activities such as music, dance or sports we realize that those who push themselves to practice regularly have the most success. Forcing ourselves to take the time to write that thank you note or letter of encouragement builds successful relationships and we have all noticed how hard work translates into more rewarding careers. Is it any wonder then that pushing ourselves to do the right things in all of our business decisions, even when they are the most difficult to do, make for the best outcomes in the long run.

Conclusion

In the words of the late American educator and author, Booker T. Washington *"Few things can help an individual more than to place responsibility on him, and to let him know that you trust him."* How much better could one sum up the sentiment of this book? The human spirit thrives in an atmosphere of trust; willing to step out in confidence, push the edges of the envelope, all in an effort to make a difference. Yes, I truly believe that people want to make a difference - for their hard work to have a positive impact on the organizations that they are involved with whether that is for employment or personal interest. Conversely, when those in positions of authority micro-manage every aspect of one's performance; it sucks the very life out of the business. Nothing is more demoralizing than the constant feeling of being under surveillance - the attitude on the part of supervisors that "I know you are going to do something wrong, and I'm going to catch you". We must ask ourselves; why do organizations allow people of such a controlling nature come to positions of prominence? I suspect there are two reasons, first that they were in need of a "fixer" and secondly, the individual was not that way when given the position in the first place.

The normal business lifecycle all but insures that any company will, at some point, face times of uncertainty and turmoil. It is at these times that help is sought from someone who can "fix" the problem, an individual or team who can right the ship so-to-speak. Off-times this option is only considered when the situation is dire and the company is on the precipice of extinction. This condition is not confined only to the business arena, it has manifested itself in the geo-political world as well when societal unrest becomes so disruptive that countries are willing to accept ruthless dictators as long as they are able to curtail the current tide of unruly protests. Human nature is such that we frequently approach these situations with blinders on, refusing to acknowledge the fact that our once tried-and-true business model is no longer tenable in the current marketplace. By the time company executives or board members awaken to the impending doom the situation is urgent and in need of drastic corrective measures. In order to implement these types of dramatic changes it is necessary to employ the type of hard-driving individual who has a track record of getting things done - the kind of person who will kick butt and take names. We are willing to turn a blind eye to the situation as long as they fix the problem now!

The ironic part of this entire discussion is that at such a critical moment this is the absolute right thing to do. Just as I mentioned at the outset of this book, in an emergency situation there is no time for consensus building or participative management. Plans must be made and executed effectively and efficiently as a matter of survival. When your company is on the edge of the cliff, it is of the utmost importance to insure that every aspect of the plan is completed on time and as planned. Consequently, checklists and follow-up are the order of the day even if they are burdensome, because there is no room for error. Discussions as to whether the chosen plan is the best plan are only obstacles to success; it has been my experience that a well-executed mediocre plan will outperform a better plan that is either slow to implement or poorly deployed. One caveat to this discussion however, if employees are well informed and understand the severity of the circumstances they will do a much better job making it happen even in this situation. By trusting your team enough to lay all the cards on the table they will come to the rescue like white knights saving a damsel in distress, people will fight for a cause. Nevertheless, most business experts will acknowledge the fact that the same team that pulls a company back from the edge is not the same one to move the company forward once the problem has been averted. By maintaining this posture of crisis management longer than necessary an organization can begin to drift back into a state of lackluster performance as employees grow fatigued by the continuance of emergency tactics. It takes an entirely different skill-set to shift gears and enter into a phase of renewed initiative and growth.

It is rare that the same individuals contain both, yet during the critical stage (often at least a few years) many middle management positions will have been staffed with individuals that possess the same autocratic management style desired to fix the problem. These very capable individuals become organizationally entrenched and turn out to be barriers to change as the company attempts to move forward in a more entrepreneurial fashion. The new direction seems foreign to them resulting in skewed messages or misinterpretation as they are forced out of their comfort zone or worse yet, they undermine the transition in an effort to protect their job. Frustration grows as team members begin to sense a certain incongruence between the message they are hearing from corporate executives and the reality of what they are experiencing in their day-to-day operations.

When deciding to deploy corrective measures of such magnitude, it would be wise to also have an exit strategy. *What happens if the plan works?* It is so easy to be focused on the problem at hand that what happens next is completely off the radar screen. Organizations should undertake such action with a clear understanding of why it is necessary, what the key issues are, how they will be addressed and what benchmarks will signify success. Only then can they understand the management needs both during and after the crisis. An exit strategy can not only put the company on track for growth sooner, but it can best utilize talent by anticipating the shift in management style that must occur moving forward.

The second reason prominent positions are sometimes staffed with autocratic controlling individuals is that they were not that way when they were initially given the position. At times this is merely the result of pre-conceived notions of what a person in that position is supposed to act like. I once worked with an individual who seemed to change personalities every time he changed job titles. When he was in a sales or staff position he was friendly, helpful and gregarious, yet when he moved to an operations position his demeanor changed drastically to demanding, controlling and authoritative. This individual's career seemed to bounce back and forth between the two job classifications and each time the same tendencies would manifest themselves. Sometimes the very traits that get someone promoted to a position of authority simply disappear as they attempt to model their personal understanding of what that job entails. Just as psychologists have suggested that children from an abusive home may have the same tendencies later in life or those from an environment of addiction may also develop an addictive tendency even though, in both cases, one would think they would do the opposite; those that have experienced bad management may very well repeat what they have encountered because this is what they understand to be the model for the position.

Of course not every reason for changing, once in the job, is quite so Freudian; sometimes it is just a matter of expediency. Not everyone who is promoted to a management position is fully prepared for the demands they will encounter. A friend of mine once told me that earlier in his career he had received a major promotion that almost doubled his salary. When he told his father about this stroke of good fortune, the father responded "if they doubled your salary, you can be sure they will more than double your workload"! Once we move through the honeymoon stage of any promotion we begin to see the magnitude of the responsibilities. As a result we are sometimes overwhelmed and look for the most expedient ways to get things done. Those things that we used to seek input for are now dispatched carte blanche. One begins to rely on their own experience or intuition when making decisions rather than involving others who may have valuable input. This not only tends to produce poor decisions, but it is terribly demoralizing to team members who are eager to share their ideas and wish to make a positive contribution of their own. There is nothing so engaging or motivating than to have someone seek your input and potentially incorporate those ideas into a grander plan. Even when an idea is not used it still fosters an atmosphere of collaboration and respect. I have always noticed that the most intelligent and accomplished people seem to be the ones that are always interested in what others have to say rather than dominate a conversation with their own opinion on the topic at hand. On occasion, I have found myself rattling on about my own interests as one more accomplished than me probes for more information, when in fact I should be sitting quietly and listening to their learned opinions. They radiate such a thirst for knowledge, one would think this would be a perfect model for how we should conduct ourselves in most business settings. Of course, there is no perfect solution to this dilemma because there will always be more things to do than we have time to do them in. But simply being aware of the potential problem and utilizing good time-management skills can result in noticeable improvement.

In conclusion, senior managers set the tone for the attitude of the entire organization and thereby shoulder the responsibility of creating a positive environment in which talented individuals can deliver exceptional results. When they exhibit a willingness to collaborate on important decisions, to value the contribution of others and to treat others with dignity and respect, they foster an atmosphere of creativity and growth. Their actions are mimicked throughout the company as they demonstrate that closed minded – dictatorial management styles are not tolerated. It then becomes the responsibility of each of us to insure that we are following suit, bringing value to the organization by challenging and energizing fellow employees to utilize their skills in innovative ways that bring credibility and success to the company.

Unquestionably, most of us have a difficult time looking in the mirror and doing an adequate job of self-evaluation. But, if we are truly concerned with the success of the organizations we are involved with, we will strive to be more open and honest with ourselves, receptive to constructive criticism and willing to take corrective measures when necessary. Our capitalist system is the best societal framework mankind has come up with since we began living in communities. The profit motive, when couched in an atmosphere of insightful governmental restraint and coupled with people oriented management styles, provides a stimulus for growth, financial stability and innovation. Business, however, can be more than just about making money; it can be about nurturing talent and invigorating the human spirit. Enthused and motivated individuals are the growth engine of progress – the kind of progress that drives economic expansion and, as a result, improved profitability. **This is the Business of Trust.**

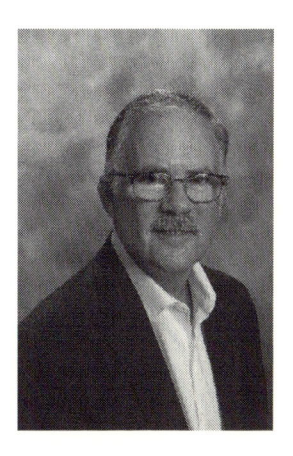

About the Author:

Ray Filasky recently retired from a career that encompassed self-employment, direct sales experience and over 25 years of various levels of managerial positions. Holding both a Bachelor's and Master's Degrees in Business Administration, his educational background and work experience have made him a staunch proponent of participative management styles and the importance of cultivating the creativity and enthusiasm of fellow co-workers. Raised on a potato farm, he was instilled early on with a strong work ethic that believes that we are each accountable for our own hard work as well as to always give our best and that the majority of individuals want to do just that, if given the chance. His deeply held Christian beliefs underpin a perspective that values ethical behavior and human dignity. It is the responsibility of any organization (at least if they wish to be successful and relevant) to cultivate an atmosphere that champions the creativity and autonomy of the individual while, at the same time, providing a clear vison of the overall objectives of the association. His desire is to influence the management style of current and future leaders in such a way that it provides a more rewarding and harmonious workplace for employees as well as the profitability necessary to sustain an ongoing business.